THIRD EDITION

RESUMES FOR

ENGINEERING CAREERS

With Sample Cover Letters

The Editors of McGraw-Hill

McGraw·Hill

*New York   Chicago   San Francisco   Lisbon   London   Madrid   Mexico City
Milan   New Delhi   San Juan   Seoul   Singapore   Sydney   Toronto*

Library of Congress Cataloging-in-Publication Data

Resumes for engineering careers / the editors of McGraw-Hill.—3rd ed.
    p.   cm. — (McGraw-Hill professional resumes series)
ISBN 0-07-144890-X (alk. paper)
1. Engineers—Employment   2. Resumes (Employment)   I. Series.

TA157.R47   2005
650.14'2—dc22   2005041569

1 2 3 4 5 6 7 8 9 0 QPD/QPD 0 9 8 7 6 5

ISBN 0-07-144890-X

McGraw-Hill books are available at special quantity discounts to use as premiums and sales promotions, or for use in corporate training programs. For more information, please write to the Director of Special Sales, Professional Publishing, McGraw-Hill, Two Penn Plaza, New York, NY 10121-2298. Or contact your local bookstore.

This book is printed on acid-free paper.

Contents

Introduction

Your resume is a piece of paper (or an electronic document) that serves to introduce you to the people who will eventually hire you. To write a thoughtful resume, you must thoroughly assess your personality, your accomplishments, and the skills you have acquired. The act of composing and submitting a resume also requires you to carefully consider the company or individual that might hire you. What are they looking for, and how can you meet their needs? This book shows you how to organize your personal information and experience into a concise and well-written resume so that your qualifications and potential as an employee will be understood easily and quickly by a complete stranger.

Writing the resume is just one step in what can be a daunting job-search process, but it is an important element in the chain of events that will lead you to your new position. While you are probably a talented, bright, and charming person, your resume may not reflect these qualities. A poorly written resume can get you nowhere; a well-written resume can land you an interview and potentially a job. A good resume can even lead the interviewer to ask you questions that will allow you to talk about your strengths and highlight the skills you can bring to a prospective employer. Even a person with very little experience can find a good job if he or she is assisted by a thoughtful and polished resume.

Lengthy, typewritten resumes are a thing of the past. Today, employers do not have the time or the patience for verbose documents; they look for tightly composed, straightforward, action-based resumes. Although a one-page resume is the norm, a two-page resume may be warranted if you have had extensive job experience or have changed careers and truly need the space to properly position yourself. If, after careful editing, you still need more than one page to present yourself, it's acceptable to use a second page. A crowded resume that's hard to read would be the worst of your choices.

Distilling your work experience, education, and interests into such a small space requires preparation and thought. This book takes you step-by-step through the process of crafting an effective resume that will stand out in today's competitive marketplace. It serves as a workbook and a place to write down your experiences, while also including the techniques you'll need to pull all the necessary elements together. In the following pages, you'll find many examples of resumes that are specific to your area of interest. Study them for inspiration and find what appeals to you. There are a variety of ways to organize and present your information; inside, you'll find several that will be suitable to your needs. Good luck landing the job of your dreams!

The Elements of an Effective Resume

An effective resume is composed of information that employers are most interested in knowing about a prospective job applicant. This information is conveyed by a few essential elements. The following is a list of elements that are found in most resumes—some essential, some optional. Later in this chapter, we will further examine the role of each of these elements in the makeup of your resume.

- Heading

- Objective and/or Keyword Section

- Work Experience

- Education

- Honors

- Activities

- Certificates and Licenses

- Publications

- Professional Memberships

- Special Skills

- Personal Information

- References

The first step in preparing your resume is to gather information about yourself and your past accomplishments. Later you will refine this information, rewrite it using effective language, and organize it into an attractive layout. But first, let's take a look at each of these important elements individually so you can judge their appropriateness for your resume.

Heading

Although the heading may seem to be the simplest section of your resume, be careful not to take it lightly. It is the first section your prospective employer will see, and it contains the information she or he will need to contact you. At the very least, the heading must contain your name, your home address, and, of course, a phone number where you can be reached easily.

In today's high-tech world, many of us have multiple ways that we can be contacted. You may list your e-mail address if you are reasonably sure the employer makes use of this form of communication. Keep in mind, however, that others may have access to your e-mail messages if you send them from an account provided by your current company. If this is a concern, do not list your work e-mail address on your resume. If you are able to take calls at your current place of business, you should include your work number, because most employers will attempt to contact you during typical business hours.

If you have voice mail or a reliable answering machine at home or at work, list its number in the heading and make sure your greeting is professional and clear. Always include at least one phone number in your heading, even if it is a temporary number, where a prospective employer can leave a message.

You might have a dozen different ways to be contacted, but you do not need to list all of them. Confine your numbers or addresses to those that are the easiest for the prospective employer to use and the simplest for you to retrieve.

Objective

When seeking a specific career path, it is important to list a job or career objective on your resume. This statement helps employers know the direction you see yourself taking, so they can determine whether your goals are in line with those of their organization and the position available. Normally, an objective is one to two sentences long. Its contents will vary depending on your career field, goals, and personality. The objective can be specific or general, but it should always be to the point. See the sample resumes in this book for examples.

If you are planning to use this resume online, or you suspect your potential employer is likely to scan your resume, you will want to include a "keyword" in the objective. This allows a prospective employer, searching hundreds of resumes for a specific skill or position objective, to locate the keyword and find your resume. In essence, a keyword is what's "hot" in your particular field at a given time. It's a buzzword, a shorthand way of getting a particular message across at a glance. For example, if you are a lawyer, your objective might state your desire to work in the area of corporate litigation. In this case, someone searching for the keyword "corporate litigation" will pull up your resume and know that you want to plan, research, and present cases at trial on behalf of the corporation. If your objective states that you "desire a challenging position in systems design," the keyword is "systems design," an industry-specific shorthand way of saying that you want to be involved in assessing the need for, acquiring, and implementing high-technology systems. These are keywords and every industry has them, so it's becoming more and more important to include a few in your resume. (You may need to conduct additional research to make sure you know what keywords are most likely to be used in your desired industry, profession, or situation.)

There are many resume and job-search sites online. Like most things in the online world, they vary a great deal in quality. Use your discretion. If you plan to apply for jobs online or advertise your availability this way, you will want to design a scannable resume. This type of resume uses a format that can be easily scanned into a computer and added to a database. Scanning allows a prospective employer to use keywords to quickly review each applicant's experience and skills, and (in the event that there are many candidates for the job) to keep your resume for future reference.

Many people find that it is worthwhile to create two or more versions of their basic resume. You may want an intricately designed resume on high-quality paper to mail or hand out *and* a resume that is designed to be scanned into a computer and saved on a database or an online job site. You can even create a resume in ASCII text to e-mail to prospective employers. For further information, you may wish to refer to the *Guide to Internet Job Searching*, by Frances Roehm and Margaret Dikel, updated and published every other year by McGraw-Hill. This excellent book contains helpful and detailed information about formatting a resume for Internet use. To get you started, in Chapter 3 we have included a list of things to keep in mind when creating electronic resumes.

Although it is usually a good idea to include an objective, in some cases this element is not necessary. The goal of the objective statement is to provide the employer with an idea of where you see yourself going in the field. However, if you are uncertain of the exact nature of the job you seek, including an objective that is too specific could result in your not being considered for a host of perfectly acceptable positions. If you decide not to use an objective heading in your resume, you should definitely incorporate the information that would be conveyed in the objective into your cover letter.

Work Experience

Work experience is arguably the most important element of them all. Unless you are a recent graduate or former homemaker with little or no relevant work experience, your current and former positions will provide the central focus of the resume. You will want this section to be as complete and carefully constructed as possible. By thoroughly examining your work experience, you can get to the heart of your accomplishments and present them in a way that demonstrates and highlights your qualifications.

If you are just entering the workforce, your resume will probably focus on your education, but you should also include information on your work or volunteer experiences. Although you will have less information about work experience than a person who has held multiple positions or is advanced in his or her career, the amount of information is not what is most important in this section. How the information is presented and what it says about you as a worker and a person are what really count.

As you create this section of your resume, remember the need for accuracy. Include all the necessary information about each of your jobs, including your job title, dates of employment, name of your employer, city, state, responsibilities, special projects you handled, and accomplishments. Be sure to list only accomplishments for which you were directly responsible. And don't be alarmed if you haven't participated in or worked on special projects, because this section may not be relevant to certain jobs.

The most common way to list your work experience is in *reverse chronological order*. In other words, start with your most recent job and work your way backward. This way, your prospective employer sees your current (and often most important) position before considering your past employment. Your most recent position, if it's the most important in terms of responsibilities and relevance to the job for which you are applying, should also be the one that includes the most information as compared to your previous positions.

Even if the work itself seems unrelated to your proposed career path, you should list any job or experience that will help sell your talents. If you were promoted or given greater responsibilities or commendations, be sure to mention the fact.

The following worksheet is provided to help you organize your experiences in the working world. It will also serve as an excellent resource to refer to when updating your resume in the future.

WORK EXPERIENCE

Job One:

Job Title _____

Dates _____

Employer _____

City, State _____

Major Duties _____

_____

_____

_____

_____

_____

_____

_____

Special Projects _____

_____

_____

_____

Accomplishments _____

_____

_____

_____

_____

_____

Job Two:

Job Title _____

Dates _____

Employer _____

City, State _____

Major Duties _____

_____

_____

_____

_____

_____

_____

Special Projects _____

_____

_____

_____

Accomplishments _____

_____

_____

_____

_____

_____

_____

_____

Job Three:

Job Title _____

Dates _____

Employer _____

City, State _____

Major Duties _____

_____

_____

_____

_____

_____

_____

_____

Special Projects _____

_____

_____

_____

Accomplishments _____

_____

_____

_____

_____

_____

_____

_____

_____

Job Four:

Job Title _____

Dates _____

Employer _____

City, State _____

Major Duties _____

_____

_____

_____

_____

_____

_____

_____

_____

Special Projects _____

_____

_____

_____

Accomplishments _____

_____

_____

_____

_____

_____

_____

_____

_____

Education

Education is usually the second most important element of a resume. Your educational background is often a deciding factor in an employer's decision to interview you. Highlight your accomplishments in school as much as you did those accomplishments at work. If you are looking for your first professional job, your education or life experience will be your greatest asset because your related work experience will be minimal. In this case, the education section becomes the most important means of selling yourself.

Include in this section all the degrees or certificates you have received; your major or area of concentration; all of the honors you earned; and any relevant activities you participated in, organized, or chaired. Again, list your most recent schooling first. If you have completed graduate-level work, begin with that and work your way back through your undergraduate education. If you have completed college, you generally should not list your high-school experience; do so only if you earned special honors, you had a grade point average that was much better than the norm, or this was your highest level of education.

If you have completed a large number of credit hours in a subject that may be relevant to the position you are seeking but did not obtain a degree, you may wish to list the hours or classes you completed. Keep in mind, however, that you may be asked to explain why you did not finish the program. If you are currently in school, list the degree, certificate, or license you expect to obtain and the projected date of completion.

The following worksheet will help you gather the information you need for this section of your resume.

EDUCATION

School One _____

Major or Area of Concentration _____

Degree _____

Dates _____

School Two _____

Major or Area of Concentration _____

Degree _____

Dates _____

Honors

If you include an honors section in your resume, you should highlight any awards, honors, or memberships in honorary societies that you have received. (You may also incorporate this information into your education section.) Often, the honors are academic in nature, but this section also may be used for special achievements in sports, clubs, or other school activities. Always include the name of the organization awarding the honor and the date(s) received. Use the following worksheet to help you gather your information.

HONORS

Honor One _____

Awarding Organization _____

Date(s) _____

Honor Two _____

Awarding Organization _____

Date(s) _____

Honor Three _____

Awarding Organization _____

Date(s) _____

Honor Four _____

Awarding Organization _____

Date(s) _____

Honor Five _____

Awarding Organization _____

Date(s) _____

Activities

Perhaps you have been active in different organizations or clubs; often an employer will look at such involvement as evidence of initiative, dedication, and good social skills. Examples of your ability to take a leading role in a group should be included on a resume, if you can provide them. The activities section of your resume should present neighborhood and community activities, volunteer positions, and so forth. In general, you may want to avoid listing any organization whose name indicates the race, creed, sex, age, marital status, sexual orientation, or nation of origin of its members because this could expose you to discrimination. Use the following worksheet to list the specifics of your activities.

ACTIVITIES

Organization/Activity _____

Accomplishments _____

_____

_____

Organization/Activity _____

Accomplishments _____

_____

_____

Organization/Activity _____

Accomplishments _____

_____

_____

As your work experience grows through the years, your school activities and honors will carry less weight and be emphasized less in your resume. Eventually, you will probably list only your degree and any major honors received. As time goes by, your job performance and the experience you've gained become the most important elements in your resume, which should change to reflect this.

Certificates and Licenses

If your chosen career path requires specialized training, you may already have certificates or licenses. You should list these if the job you are seeking requires them and you, of course, have acquired them. If you have applied for a license but have not yet received it, use the phrase "application pending."

License requirements vary by state. If you have moved or are planning to relocate to another state, check with that state's board or licensing agency for all licensing requirements.

Always make sure that all of the information you list is completely accurate. Locate copies of your certificates and licenses, and check the exact date and name of the accrediting agency. Use the following worksheet to organize the necessary information.

CERTIFICATES AND LICENSES

Name of License _____

Licensing Agency _____

Date Issued _____

Name of License _____

Licensing Agency _____

Date Issued _____

Name of License _____

Licensing Agency _____

Date Issued _____

Publications

Some professions strongly encourage or even require that you publish. If you have written, coauthored, or edited any books, articles, professional papers, or works of a similar nature that pertain to your field, you will definitely want to include this element. Remember to list the date of publication and the publisher's name, and specify whether you were the sole author or a coauthor. Book, magazine, or journal titles are generally italicized, while the titles of articles within a larger publication appear in quotes. (Check with your reference librarian for more about the appropriate way to present this information.) For scientific or research papers, you will need to give the date, place, and audience to whom the paper was presented.

Use the following worksheet to help you gather the necessary information about your publications.

PUBLICATIONS

Title and Type (Note, Article, etc.) _____

Title of Publication (Journal, Book, etc.) _____

Publisher _____

Date Published _____

Title and Type (Note, Article, etc.) _____

Title of Publication (Journal, Book, etc.) _____

Publisher _____

Date Published _____

Title and Type (Note, Article, etc.) _____

Title of Publication (Journal, Book, etc.) _____

Publisher _____

Date Published _____

Professional Memberships

Another potential element in your resume is a section listing professional memberships. Use this section to describe your involvement in professional associations, unions, and similar organizations. It is to your advantage to list any professional memberships that pertain to the job you are seeking. Many employers see your membership as representative of your desire to stay up-to-date and connected in your field. Include the dates of your involvement and whether you took part in any special activities or held any offices within the organization. Use the following worksheet to organize your information.

PROFESSIONAL MEMBERSHIPS

Name of Organization _____

Office(s) Held_____

Activities _____

Dates _____

Name of Organization _____

Office(s) Held_____

Activities _____

Dates _____

Name of Organization _____

Office(s) Held_____

Activities _____

Dates _____

Name of Organization _____

Office(s) Held_____

Activities _____

Dates _____

Special Skills

The special skills section of your resume is the place to mention any special abilities you have that relate to the job you are seeking. You can use this element to present certain talents or experiences that are not necessarily a part of your education or work experience. Common examples include fluency in a foreign language, extensive travel abroad, or knowledge of a particular computer application. "Special skills" can encompass a wide range of talents, and this section can be used creatively. However, for each skill you list, you should be able to describe how it would be a direct asset in the type of work you're seeking because employers may ask just that in an interview. If you can't think of a way to do this, it may be extraneous information.

Personal Information

Some people include personal information on their resumes. This is generally not recommended, but you might wish to include it if you think that something in your personal life, such as a hobby or talent, has some bearing on the position you are seeking. This type of information is often referred to at the beginning of an interview, when it may be used as an icebreaker. Of course, personal information regarding your age, marital status, race, religion, or sexual orientation should never appear on your resume as personal information. It should be given only in the context of memberships and activities, and only when doing so would not expose you to discrimination.

References

References are not usually given on the resume itself, but a prospective employer needs to know that you have references who may be contacted if necessary. All you need to include is a single sentence at the end of the resume: "References are available upon request," or even simply, "References available." Have a reference list ready—your interviewer may ask to see it! Contact each person on the list ahead of time to see whether it is all right for you to use him or her as a reference. This way, the person has a chance to think about what to say *before* the call occurs. This helps ensure that you will obtain the best reference possible.

Chapter 2

Writing Your Resume

Now that you have gathered the information for each section of your resume, it's time to write it out in a way that will get the attention of the reviewer—hopefully, your future employer! The language you use in your resume will affect its success, so you must be careful and conscientious. Translate the facts you have gathered into the active, precise language of resume writing. You will be aiming for a resume that keeps the reader's interest and highlights your accomplishments in a concise and effective way.

Resume writing is unlike any other form of writing. Although your seventh-grade composition teacher would not approve, the rules of punctuation and sentence building are often completely ignored. Instead, you should try for a functional, direct writing style that focuses on the use of verbs and other words that imply action on your part. Writing with action words and strong verbs characterizes you to potential employers as an energetic, active person, someone who completes tasks and achieves results from his or her work. Resumes that do not make use of action words can sound passive and stale. These resumes are not effective and do not get the attention of any employer, no matter how qualified the applicant. Choose words that display your strengths and demonstrate your initiative. The following list of commonly used verbs will help you create a strong resume:

administered	assembled
advised	assumed responsibility
analyzed	billed
arranged	built

carried out	inspected
channeled	interviewed
collected	introduced
communicated	invented
compiled	maintained
completed	managed
conducted	met with
contacted	motivated
contracted	negotiated
coordinated	operated
counseled	orchestrated
created	ordered
cut	organized
designed	oversaw
determined	performed
developed	planned
directed	prepared
dispatched	presented
distributed	produced
documented	programmed
edited	published
established	purchased
expanded	recommended
functioned as	recorded
gathered	reduced
handled	referred
hired	represented
implemented	researched
improved	reviewed

saved	supervised
screened	taught
served as	tested
served on	trained
sold	typed
suggested	wrote

Let's look at two examples that differ only in their writing style. The first resume section is ineffective because it does not use action words to accent the applicant's work experiences.

WORK EXPERIENCE
Regional Sales Manager

Manager of sales representatives from seven states. Manager of twelve food chain accounts in the East. In charge of the sales force's planned selling toward specific goals. Supervisor and trainer of new sales representatives. Consulting for customers in the areas of inventory management and quality control.

Special Projects: Coordinator and sponsor of annual Food Industry Seminar.

Accomplishments: Monthly regional volume went up 25 percent during my tenure while, at the same time, a proper sales/cost ratio was maintained. Customer-company relations were improved.

In the following paragraph, we have rewritten the same section using action words. Notice how the tone has changed. It now sounds stronger and more active. This person accomplished goals and really *did* things.

WORK EXPERIENCE
Regional Sales Manager

Managed sales representatives from seven states. Oversaw twelve food chain accounts in the eastern United States. Directed the sales force in planned selling toward specific goals. Supervised and trained new sales representatives. Counseled customers in the areas of inventory management and quality control. Coordinated and sponsored the annual Food Industry Seminar. Increased monthly regional volume by 25 percent and helped to improve customer-company relations during my tenure.

One helpful way to construct the work experience section is to make use of your actual job descriptions—the written duties and expectations your employers have for a person in your current or former position. Job descriptions are rarely written in proper resume language, so you will have to rework them, but they do include much of the information necessary to create this section of your resume. If you have access to job descriptions for your former positions, you can use the details to construct an action-oriented paragraph. Often, your human resources department can provide a job description for your current position.

The following is an example of a typical human resources job description, followed by a rewritten version of the same description employing action words and specific details about the job. Again, pay attention to the style of writing instead of the content, as the details of your own experience will be unique.

WORK EXPERIENCE
Public Administrator I

Responsibilities: Coordinate and direct public services to meet the needs of the nation, state, or community. Analyze problems; work with special committees and public agencies; recommend solutions to governing bodies.

Aptitudes and Skills: Ability to relate to and communicate with people; solve complex problems through analysis; plan, organize, and implement policies and programs. Knowledge of political systems, financial management, personnel administration, program evaluation, and organizational theory.

WORK EXPERIENCE
Public Administrator I

Wrote pamphlets and conducted discussion groups to inform citizens of legislative processes and consumer issues. Organized and supervised 25 interviewers. Trained interviewers in effective communication skills.

After you have written out your resume, you are ready to begin the next important step: assembly and layout.

Chapter 3

Assembly and Layout

At this point, you've gathered all the necessary information for your resume and rewritten it in language that will impress your potential employers. Your next step is to assemble the sections in a logical order and lay them out on the page neatly and attractively to achieve the desired effect: getting the interview.

Assembly

The order of the elements in a resume makes a difference in its overall effect. Clearly, you would not want to bury your name and address somewhere in the middle of the resume. Nor would you want to lead with a less important section, such as special skills. Put the elements in an order that stresses your most important accomplishments and the things that will be most appealing to your potential employer. For example, if you are new to the workforce, you will want the reviewer to read about your education and life skills before any part-time jobs you may have held for short durations. On the other hand, if you have been gainfully employed for several years and currently hold an important position in your company, you should list your work accomplishments ahead of your educational information, which has become less pertinent with time.

Certain things should always be included in your resume, but others are optional. The following list shows you which are which. You might want to use it as a checklist to be certain that you have included all of the necessary information.

Essential	**Optional**
Name	Cellular Phone Number
Address	Pager Number
Phone Number	E-Mail Address or Website Address
Work Experience	Voice Mail Number
Education	Job Objective
References Phrase	Honors
	Special Skills
	Publications
	Professional Memberships
	Activities
	Certificates and Licenses
	Personal Information
	Graphics
	Photograph

Your choice of optional sections depends on your own background and employment needs. Always use information that will put you in a favorable light—unless it's absolutely essential, avoid anything that will prompt the interviewer to ask questions about your weaknesses or something else that could be unflattering. Make sure your information is accurate and truthful. If your honors are impressive, include them in the resume. If your activities in school demonstrate talents that are necessary for the job you are seeking, allow space for a section on activities. If you are applying for a position that requires ornamental illustration, you may want to include border illustrations or graphics that demonstrate your talents in this area. If you are answering an advertisement for a job that requires certain physical traits, a photo of yourself might be appropriate. A person applying for a job as a computer programmer would *not* include a photo as part of his or her resume. Each resume is unique, just as each person is unique.

Types of Resumes

So far we have focused on the most common type of resume—the *reverse chronological* resume—in which your most recent job is listed first. This is the type of resume usually preferred by those who have to read a large number of resumes, and it is by far the most popular and widely circulated. However, this style of presentation may not be the most effective way to highlight *your* skills and accomplishments.

For example, if you are reentering the workforce after many years or are trying to change career fields, the *functional* resume may work best. This type of resume puts the focus on your achievements instead of the sequence of your work history. In the functional resume, your experience is presented through your general accomplishments and the skills you have developed in your working life.

A functional resume is assembled from the same information you gathered in Chapter 1. The main difference lies in how you organize the information. Essentially, the work experience section is divided in two, with your job duties and accomplishments constituting one section and your employers' names, cities, and states; your positions; and the dates employed making up the other. Place the first section near the top of your resume, just below your job objective (if used), and call it *Accomplishments* or *Achievements*. The second section, containing the bare essentials of your work history, should come after the accomplishments section and can be called *Employment History*, since it is a chronological overview of your former jobs.

The other sections of your resume remain the same. The work experience section is the only one affected in the functional format. By placing the section that focuses on your achievements at the beginning, you draw attention to these achievements. This puts less emphasis on where you worked and when, and more on what you did and what you are capable of doing.

If you are changing careers, the emphasis on skills and achievements is important. The identities of previous employers (who aren't part of your new career field) need to be downplayed. A functional resume can help accomplish this task. If you are reentering the workforce after a long absence, a functional resume is the obvious choice. And if you lack full-time work experience, you will need to draw attention away from this fact and put the focus on your skills and abilities. You may need to highlight your volunteer activities and part-time work. Education may also play a more important role in your resume.

The type of resume that is right for you will depend on your personal circumstances. It may be helpful to create both types and then compare them. Which one presents you in the best light? Examples of both types of resumes are included in this book. Use the sample resumes in Chapter 5 to help you decide on the content, presentation, and look of your own resume.

Resume or Curriculum Vitae?

A curriculum vitae (CV) is a longer, more detailed synopsis of your professional history, which generally runs three or more pages in length. It includes a summary of your educational and academic background as well as teaching and research experience, publications, presentations, awards, honors, affiliations, and other details. Because the purpose of the CV is different from that of the resume, many of the rules we've discussed thus far involving style and length do not apply.

A curriculum vitae is used primarily for admissions applications to graduate or professional schools, independent consulting in a variety of settings, proposals for fellowships or grants, or applications for positions in academia. As with a resume, you may need different versions of a CV for different types of positions. You should only send a CV when one is specifically requested by an employer or institution.

Like a resume, your CV should include your name, contact information, education, skills, and experience. In addition to the basics, a CV includes research and teaching experience, publications, grants and fellowships, professional associations and licenses, awards, and other information relevant to the position for which you are applying. You can follow the advice presented thus far to gather and organize your personal information.

Special Tips for Electronic Resumes

Because there are many details to consider in writing a resume that will be posted or transmitted on the Internet, or one that will be scanned into a computer when it is received, we suggest that you refer to the *Guide to Internet Job Searching*, by Frances Roehm and Margaret Dikel, as previously mentioned. However, here are some brief, general guidelines to follow if you expect your resume to be scanned into a computer.

- Use standard fonts in which none of the letters touch.

- Keep in mind that underlining, italics, and fancy scripts may not scan well.

- Use boldface and capitalization to set off elements. Again, make sure letters don't touch. Leave at least a quarter inch between lines of type.

- Keep information and elements at the left margin. Centering, columns, and even indenting may change when the resume is optically scanned.

- Do not use any lines, boxes, or graphics.

- Place the most important information at the top of the first page. If you use two pages, put "Page 1 of 2" at the bottom of the first page and put your name and "Page 2 of 2" at the top of the second page.

- List each telephone number on its own line in the header.

- Use multiple keywords or synonyms for what you do to make sure your qualifications will be picked up if a prospective employer is searching for them. Use nouns that are keywords for your profession.

- Be descriptive in your titles. For example, don't just use "assistant"; use "legal office assistant."

- Make sure the contrast between print and paper is good. Use a high-quality laser printer and white or very light colored 8½-by-11-inch paper.

- Mail a high-quality laser print or an excellent copy. Do not fold or use staples, as this might interfere with scanning. You may, however, use paper clips.

In addition to creating a resume that works well for scanning, you may want to have a resume that can be e-mailed to reviewers. Because you may not know what word processing application the recipient uses, the best format to use is ASCII text. (ASCII stands for "American Standard Code for Information Interchange.") It allows people with very different software platforms to exchange and understand information. (E-mail operates on this principle.) ASCII is a simple, text-only language, which means you can include only simple text. There can be no use of boldface, italics, or even paragraph indentations.

To create an ASCII resume, just use your normal word processing program; when finished, save it as a "text only" document. You will find this option under the "save" or "save as" command. Here is a list of things to *avoid* when crafting your electronic resume:

- Tabs. Use your space bar. Tabs will not work.

- Any special characters, such as mathematical symbols.

- Word wrap. Use hard returns (the return key) to make line breaks.

- Centering or other formatting. Align everything at the left margin.

- Bold or italic fonts. Everything will be converted to plain text when you save the file as a "text only" document.

Check carefully for any mistakes before you save the document as a text file. Spellcheck and proofread it several times; then ask someone with a keen eye to go over it again for you. Remember: the key is to keep it simple. Any attempt to make this resume pretty or decorative may result in a resume that is confusing and hard to read. After you have saved the document, you can cut and paste it into an e-mail or onto a website.

Layout for a Paper Resume

A great deal of care—and much more formatting—is necessary to achieve an attractive layout for your paper resume. There is no single appropriate layout that applies to every resume, but there are a few basic rules to follow in putting your resume on paper:

- Leave a comfortable margin on the sides, top, and bottom of the page (usually one to one and a half inches).

- Use appropriate spacing between the sections (two to three line spaces are usually adequate).

- Be consistent in the *type* of headings you use for different sections of your resume. For example, if you capitalize the heading EMPLOY-MENT HISTORY, don't use initial capitals and underlining for a section of equal importance, such as Education.

- Do not use more than one font in your resume. Stay consistent by choosing a font that is fairly standard and easy to read, and don't change it for different sections. Beware of the tendency to try to make your resume original by choosing fancy type styles; your resume may end up looking unprofessional instead of creative. Unless you are in a very creative and artistic field, you should almost always stick with tried-and-true type styles like Times New Roman and Palatino, which are often used in business writing. In the area of resume styles, conservative is usually the best way to go.

CHRONOLOGICAL RESUME

- # JORJE S. HERNANDEZ

  P.O. Box 4432 • Las Cruces, New Mexico 88011 • 505-555-0375
  jorgehernandez@xxx.com

- # OBJECTIVE

  A career track in environmental engineering with a large private or public agency.

- # WORK EXPERIENCE

  Environmental Engineer, 8/02 to present
  Brigante & Solo, Inc., Las Cruces, New Mexico
  Prepare environmental assessments and checklists, noise level predictions, ambient noise levels. Advise design engineering on environmental problems, design cross sections, estimate construction quantities. Compute wetland involvement.

  Utilities Relocation Engineer, 7/00 to 8/02
  Arizona State Department of Transportation, Phoenix, Arizona
  Work with public utilities in relocation of facilities within public right of way. Coordinate movement and develop movement agreements. Enforce clear zone.

  Engineer, 6/99 to 7/00
  Arizona State Department of Transportation, Phoenix, Arizona
  Coordinate, review, revise, and process U.S. Army Corps of Engineer permits, shorelines, flood plains, and hydraulic permits. Prepare environmental checklists, impact statements, noise level predictions, ambient noise levels, and air pollution levels. Investigate and advise for hazardous material spills, underground storage tanks, and site assessments. Prepare displays for public and court meetings.

  Review environmental documents and permits, interpret noise levels on projects, design noise barrier, and monitor and collect air quality samples. Review and approve large lots, short plats, and roadway approaches for private developers. Assemble and calibrate nine air quality control sets valued at $175,000 each.

- # EDUCATION

  B.S., Engineering, University of New Mexico, 1999
  3.8 GPA, Cum Laude.

  References will be provided on request.

FUNCTIONAL RESUME

Brooke Smith

935 Heatherstone Place, Apt. 819, Peoria, IL 61614
(309) 555-1983 • E-mail: Brookesmith@xxx.com

EDUCATION

United States Merchant Marine Academy

Degree:	Bachelor of Science, June 1997
Major:	Marine Engineering Management
Class Standing:	3.60 of 4.0 - second in class
USCG License:	Third Assistant Engineer, Steam or Diesel, Unlimited Horsepower
Commission:	Ensign, United States Naval Reserve, June 1997
Certificates:	Advanced Lifesaving/First Aid, Red Cross CPR, USCG Lifeboatman, Advanced Fire-fighting
Computer Skills:	Word Processing (WordPro, Works), Programming (True Basic), Cadkey, Spread sheets (Excel, Works), Project Scheduling Programs (Primavera), Internet, Netscape Composer, Freelance Graphics, Lotus Notes

WORK EXPERIENCE

Repair Process Engineer, **Caterpillar, Inc.**
Member of a self-directed work team developing best practice repair processes for a Caterpillar dealership's service department. Contributed to design of the user interface for the future service information delivery system. Responsible for creating a Service Operations Audit for the 793C wheel station rebuild procedure. Develop best practice rebuild standards for Caterpillar components. Attended an Applied Failure Analysis class (July '97 to present)

Shipboard Training
Sailed for one year as a Junior Engineering Officer aboard six different U.S. flag vessels. Completed a twenty credit independent study on various shipboard engineering systems. Assisted in maintenance and operation aboard both steam and diesel ships.

Industry Internship, **Vart, Mathews and Co., Hong Kong**
Aided in hull, machinery, and cargo surveys. Assisted during survey of damaged auxiliary engines in Chiwan, P.R.C. Attended joint survey of hull collision with classification society surveyors, admiralty lawyer, and P&I representative (six weeks - Oct. '96)

LEADERSHIP EXPERIENCE

• President of Society of Women Engineers for Kings Point Chapter
• Regimental Alumni Liaison Officer - Worked with senior industry alumni to enhance alumni/midshipmen

AWARDS

• All-American Scholar Collegiate Award - Selected by Dean for outstanding work and academic achievement during college career
• Frank Cashin Award - Scholarship for promoting careers in solid waste management and energy production
• Academic Achievement Awards - Dean's List (4 yrs.), Sea Year Excellence Ribbon for outstanding performance, Best Electrical Engineering Student

- Always try to fit your resume on one page. If you are having trouble with this, you may be trying to say too much. Edit out any repetitive or unnecessary information, and shorten descriptions of earlier jobs where possible. Ask a friend you trust for feedback on what seems unnecessary or unimportant. For example, you may have included too many optional sections. Today, with the prevalence of the personal computer as a tool, there is no excuse for a poorly laid out resume. Experiment with variations until you are pleased with the result.

Remember that a resume is not an autobiography. Too much information will only get in the way. The more compact your resume, the easier it will be to review. If a person who is swamped with resumes looks at yours, catches the main points, and then calls you for an interview to fill in some of the details, your resume has already accomplished its task. A clear and concise resume makes for a happy reader and a good impression.

There are times when, despite extensive editing, the resume simply cannot fit on one page. In this case, the resume should be laid out on two pages in such a way that neither clarity nor appearance is compromised. Each page of a two-page resume should be marked clearly: the first should indicate "Page 1 of 2," and the second should include your name and the page number, for example, "Julia Ramirez—Page 2 of 2." The pages should then be paper-clipped together. You may use a smaller type size (in the same font as the body of your resume) for the page numbers. Place them at the bottom of page one and the top of page two. Again, spend the time now to experiment with the layout until you find one that looks good to you.

Always show your final layout to other people and ask them what they like or dislike about it, and what impresses them most when they read your resume. Make sure that their responses are the same as what you want to elicit from your prospective employer. If they aren't the same, you should continue to make changes until the necessary information is emphasized.

Proofreading

After you have finished typing the master copy of your resume and before you have it copied or printed, thoroughly check it for typing and spelling errors. Do not place all your trust in your computer's spellcheck function. Use an old editing trick and read the whole resume backward—start at the end and read it right to left and bottom to top. This can help you see the small errors or inconsistencies that are easy to overlook. Take time to do it right because a single error on a document this important can cause the reader to judge your attention to detail in a harsh light.

Have several people look at the finished resume just in case you've missed an error. Don't try to take a shortcut; not having an unbiased set of eyes examine your resume now could mean embarrassment later. Even experienced editors can easily overlook their own errors. Be thorough and conscientious with your proofreading so your first impression is a perfect one.

We have included the following rules of capitalization and punctuation to assist you in the final stage of creating your resume. Remember that resumes often require use of a shorthand style of writing that may include sentences without periods and other stylistic choices that break the standard rules of grammar. Be consistent in each section and throughout the whole resume with your choices.

RULES OF CAPITALIZATION

- Capitalize proper nouns, such as names of schools, colleges, and universities; names of companies; and brand names of products.

- Capitalize major words in the names and titles of books, tests, and articles that appear in the body of your resume.

- Capitalize words in major section headings of your resume.

- Do not capitalize words just because they seem important.

- When in doubt, consult a style manual such as *Words into Type* (Prentice Hall) or *The Chicago Manual of Style* (The University of Chicago Press). Your local library can help you locate these and other reference books. Many computer programs also have grammar help sections.

RULES OF PUNCTUATION

- Use commas to separate words in a series.

- Use a semicolon to separate series of words that already include commas within the series. (For an example, see the first rule of capitalization.)

- Use a semicolon to separate independent clauses that are not joined by a conjunction.

- Use a period to end a sentence.

- Use a colon to show that examples or details follow that will expand or amplify the preceding phrase.

- Avoid the use of dashes.

- Avoid the use of brackets.

- If you use any punctuation in an unusual way in your resume, be consistent in its use.

- Whenever you are uncertain, consult a style manual.

Putting Your Resume in Print

You will need to buy high-quality paper for your printer before you print your finished resume. Regular office paper is not good enough for resumes; the reviewer will probably think it looks flimsy and cheap. Go to an office supply store or copy shop and select a high-quality bond paper that will make a good first impression. Select colors like white, off-white, or possibly a light gray. In some industries, a pastel may be acceptable, but be sure the color and feel of the paper make a subtle, positive statement about you. Nothing in the choice of paper should be loud or unprofessional.

If your computer printer does not reproduce your resume properly and produces smudged or stuttered type, either ask to borrow a friend's or take your disk (or a clean original) to a printer or copy shop for high-quality copying. If you anticipate needing a large number of copies, taking your resume to a copy shop or a printer is probably the best choice.

Hold a sheet of your unprinted bond paper up to the light. If it has a watermark, you will want to point this out to the person helping you with copies; the printing should be done so that the reader can read the print and see the watermark the right way up. Check each copy for smudges or streaks. This is the time to be a perfectionist—the results of your careful preparation will be well worth it.

Chapter 4

The Cover Letter

Once your resume has been assembled, laid out, and printed to your satisfaction, the next and final step before distribution is to write your cover letter. Though there may be instances where you deliver your resume in person, you will usually send it through the mail or online. Resumes sent through the mail always need an accompanying letter that briefly introduces you and your resume. The purpose of the cover letter is to get a potential employer to read your resume, just as the purpose of the resume is to get that same potential employer to call you for an interview.

Like your resume, your cover letter should be clean, neat, and direct. A cover letter usually includes the following information:

1. Your name and address (unless it already appears on your personal letterhead) and your phone number(s); see item 7.

2. The date.

3. The name and address of the person and company to whom you are sending your resume.

4. The salutation ("Dear Mr." or "Dear Ms." followed by the person's last name, or "To Whom It May Concern" if you are answering a blind ad).

5. An opening paragraph explaining why you are writing (for example, in response to an ad, as a follow-up to a previous meeting, at the suggestion of someone you both know) and indicating that you are interested in whatever job is being offered.

6. One or more paragraphs that tell why you want to work for the company and what qualifications and experiences you can bring to the position. This is a good place to mention some detail about

that particular company that makes you want to work for them; this shows that you have done some research before applying.

7. A final paragraph that closes the letter and invites the reviewer to contact you for an interview. This can be a good place to tell the potential employer which method would be best to use when contacting you. Be sure to give the correct phone number and a good time to reach you, if that is important. You may mention here that your references are available upon request.

8. The closing ("Sincerely" or "Yours truly") followed by your signature in a dark ink, with your name typed under it.

Your cover letter should include all of this information and be no longer than one page in length. The language used should be polite, businesslike, and to the point. Don't attempt to tell your life story in the cover letter; a long and cluttered letter will serve only to annoy the reader. Remember that you need to mention only a few of your accomplishments and skills in the cover letter. The rest of your information is available in your resume. If your cover letter is a success, your resume will be read and all pertinent information reviewed by your prospective employer.

Producing the Cover Letter

Cover letters should always be individualized because they are always written to specific individuals and companies. Never use a form letter for your cover letter or copy it as you would a resume. Each cover letter should be unique, and as personal and lively as possible. (Of course, once you have written and rewritten your first cover letter until you are satisfied with it, you can certainly use similar wording in subsequent letters. You may want to save a template on your computer for future reference.) Keep a hard copy of each cover letter so you know exactly what you wrote in each one.

There are sample cover letters in Chapter 6. Use them as models or for ideas of how to assemble and lay out your own cover letters. Remember that every letter is unique and depends on the particular circumstances of the individual writing it and the job for which he or she is applying.

After you have written your cover letter, proofread it as thoroughly as you did your resume. Again, spelling or punctuation errors are a sure sign of carelessness, and you don't want that to be a part of your first impression on a prospective employer. This is no time to trust your spellcheck function. Even after going through a spelling and grammar check, your cover letter should be carefully proofread by at least one other person.

Print the cover letter on the same quality bond paper you used for your resume. Remember to sign it, using a good dark-ink pen. Handle the letter and resume carefully to avoid smudging or wrinkling, and mail them together in an appropriately sized envelope. Many stores sell matching envelopes to coordinate with your choice of bond paper.

Keep an accurate record of all resumes you send out and the results of each mailing. This record can be kept on your computer, in a calendar or notebook, or on file cards. Knowing when a resume is likely to have been received will keep you on track as you make follow-up phone calls.

About a week after mailing resumes and cover letters to potential employers, contact them by telephone. Confirm that your resume arrived and ask whether an interview might be possible. Be sure to record the name of the person you spoke to and any other information you gleaned from the conversation. It is wise to treat the person answering the phone with a great deal of respect; sometimes the assistant or receptionist has the ear of the person doing the hiring.

You should make a great impression with the strong, straightforward resume and personalized cover letter you have just created. We wish you every success in securing the career of your dreams!

Sample Resumes

This chapter contains dozens of sample resumes for people pursuing a wide variety of jobs and careers in engineering.

There are many different styles of resumes in terms of graphic layout and presentation of information. These samples represent people with varying amounts of education and experience. Use them as models for your own resume. Choose one resume or borrow elements from several different resumes to help you construct your own.

Brenda Harwood

26587 S.E. Wynona Drive
Casa Grande, Arizona 85223
(602) 555-2910
brendaharwood@xxx.com

PROFESSIONAL GOAL

To work in the drafting department of a mechanical engineering firm.

EXPERIENCE

Hyster Company, Casa Grande, Arizona
Drafter
May 2001 to present
Skilled in general production and maintenance drafting, cost-reduction research, and design-phase drafting. Work closely with designers to refine plans. Assist senior drafters with checking of drawings, preparing and releasing engineering change notices, managing department inventory, and monitoring production lists.

Engineering Assistant
July 1999 to May 2001
Assisted engineers with preparing detailed instructions for drafting department, including product design specifications, material specifications, and documentation. Consulted with drafters on design and engineering changes. Maintained detailed records of all interdepartmental communications for each specific project.

EDUCATION

Arizona State University
Mechanical Drawing/Industrial Design
B.S., 1999
Won honorable mention in competition for the design of a small-scale turbine.

REFERENCES AVAILABLE ON REQUEST

DARRYL H. WYNSTON

944 WEST SASKA BOULEVARD
BRIDGEPORT, ALABAMA 35740
(205) 555-3985
DARRYLWYNSTON@XXX.COM

OBJECTIVE

To work as a mechanical designer or drafter for a company that offers professional advancement.

EXPERIENCE

Senior Drafter
Bennington Mechanics Handling Corp., Montgomery, Alabama
5/02–present
Prepare primary and secondary concept layouts, component layouts, complex assembly drawings, and parts drawings. Prepare and release engineering change notices and production lists.

Product Engineering Drafter
General Metals Products, Montgomery, Alabama
6/96–5/02
Drafted architectural sheet metal products designs to customer specifications. Checked mechanical drawings for accuracy and precision.
Maintained drafting files for product engineering department.

ACCOMPLISHMENTS

- Used Computervision CADD System for design and layout work on a new power shift transmission.
- Developed prototype for H350-2LX noise reduction feature for major engine product.
- Experienced with CS-4x Revision 6.2b, 3-D, and solids.
- Computervision CADD operator 7/97–6/02.
- AutoCAD operator 6/02–present.

EDUCATION

Major in Mechanical Engineering
Montgomery Regional Technical Institute
9/94–6/96
Completed 108 credit hours toward B.S. degree.

REFERENCES

Available on request.

TERRY WILKINS, JR.

132 East Park Street • Jacksonville, Arkansas 72076 • (501) 555-0983 • terrywilkins@xxx.com

PROFESSIONAL OBJECTIVE

Seeking a position of responsibility in mechanical engineering. Willing to relocate.

PROFILE OF QUALIFICATIONS

Offering over 13 years of professional experience in mechanical engineering, with particular emphasis in:
- Dimension checking
- Material specifications
- Bills of materials
- Engineering records
- Layout/drawing
- Manufacturing processes
- Interdepartmental communication
- Documentation
- Metric drafting standards
- Computer-aided design and drafting

EDUCATION

Associate of Applied Science in Mechanical Drafting Technology, 1991
Little Rock Central Community College, Little Rock, Arkansas

Bachelor of Arts in History, 1985
University of Arkansas, Little Rock

RELATED CAREER HIGHLIGHTS

Jepson Corporation, Jacksonville, Arkansas
Engineering Change Notice Checker: 2002–present
Responsible for checking all engineering drawings for dimensional accuracy, correct material specifications, correct drafting procedures, and accuracy of accompanying bills of material. Maintain scheduled release dates and ensure that all production processes can be carried out expeditiously.

Engineering Draftsman: 1992–2002
Prepared layouts and drawings of new and existing industrial truck products. Work included component layouts, details, general arrangement drawings, and more. Consulted with departmental engineers and purchasing personnel. Accompanied work with documentation.

U.S. Department of Transportation, Little Rock, Arkansas
Engineering Aide (GS-3): 1991–1992
Assisted departmental engineers with drafting and documentation.

REFERENCES AVAILABLE

KEVIN SHANNON

P.O. Box 231, Bakersfield, CA 93301 (805) 555-9721
kevinshannon@xxx.com

OBJECTIVE

Relocating to Los Angeles; seeking challenging employment with industrial engineering department of a large manufacturing company.

EDUCATION

Continuing education coursework (36 hours)
Bakersfield Technical College, 1998–2003
A.A.S., Applied Engineering, 1994
College of Applied Technology, Los Angeles

EXPERIENCE

Industrial Manufacturing, Inc., Bakersfield, CA
Departmental Coordinator, Parts Engineering/December 2004–present
Assistant Supervisor/1999–2004
Engineering Aide/1994–1999

- Named National Coordinator for corporation's P.A.R. system (Parts Action Request), which was an internal method of relaying information to manufacturer, purchasing, and others.
- Instrumental in procedural change, using engineering drawings in lieu of sketches for the installation of customer-requested options not found on standard bills of material.
- Approved or rejected engineering design variation requests, ensuring that appropriate changes complied with specifications and structural requirements.
- Provided bills of material, worked with component vendors to secure special parts inventory, and compiled installation layouts.
- Trained new employees in engineering drafting practices and standards.
- Coordinated employee retraining program through local technical college.
- Developed and implemented safety program that resulted in a 35 percent decrease in on-the-job injuries.

REFERENCES AVAILABLE

SUSAN B. WATERS-LEVY

Current Address (until May 30):   **Permanent Address:**
3329 West 52nd Avenue   P.O. Box 15384
Denton, Texas 77402   San Antonio, Texas 78231
(713) 555-2975   susanwaters-levy@xxx.com

OBJECTIVE:

Electronic engineering position involving design, manufacture, and testing of digital-control systems.

EDUCATION:

B.S.E.E. (May 2005), West Texas State University, Canyonville
E.E. GPA, 4.0; Cumulative GPA, 3.56. Dean's List.

RELATED EXPERIENCE:

Laboratory Technician/Research Assistant, Department of Electrical Engineering. 2002–2004.
> Worked with experimental microelectronics in conjunction with research efforts of department faculty. Assisted lower-division students in electronics laboratory with development and testing of microprocessors, chips, and probes. Prepared analyses of micron chips fabricated in the lab for inclusion in published report.

Electronics Repair, Self-employed. 2001–2004.
> Operated small business in electronics repair servicing of computers, video recorders, and small electronic appliances.

RELEVANT COURSEWORK:

Ultrasonic and frequency control
Telemetry and guidance
Instrumentation and measurement
Industrial electronics applications
Systems, manufacturing, and cybernetics

COLLEGE HONORS/ACTIVITIES:

- President, Tau Beta Phi Honor Society
- President, IEEE West Texas State University Student Chapter
- Lab Technician of the Year Award, Department of Electrical Engineering
- Founding member, On Board, computer programmers club at WTSU

OTHER WORK EXPERIENCE:

Counter Clerk, Denton Video Rental. 2000–2002
Cook, Bob's Big Boy Burgers. 1998–2000.

REFERENCES ON REQUEST

RAY-DEAN BENNETT
15543 Framington Lane
Walnut Creek, CA 94595
(415) 555-0928
ray-deanbennett@xxx.com

PROFESSIONAL OBJECTIVE
Design engineering in robotics automation for manufacturing.

EDUCATION
B.S.M.E., Mechanical Engineering, California Institute of Technology, 2003
B.S.E.E., Electrical Engineering, California Institute of Technology, 2002

EXPERIENCE/SKILLS
- Strong mechanical and electrical engineering background, with course and lab emphasis in robotics and production-related problem solving.
- Extra coursework in heat sensing, CAD/CAM design, electronic control systems, computer programming (COBOL, PASCAL, BASIC, C++), and image-enhancing technology.
- Won regional mechanical engineering competition for design of robotics manufacturing station for production of small motor.
- Extensive knowledge of automotive mechanics and related machinery.
- Worked in family-owned automotive repair shop for 8 years, including complete engine rebuilding and overhaul.
- Experienced with use of personal computers for design, word processing, database management, and spreadsheet functions.

MEMBERSHIPS
Student chapters of the IEEE and the IAME
Tau Kappa Epsilon's Honor Society

EMPLOYMENT HISTORY
Bennett's Auto Experts, Engine Mechanic, 2000–2002

REFERENCES
Available upon request

Warren Owen Pierce

12 Boxwood Lane
Oakwood, Illinois 60335
(815) 555-2368
warrenowenpierce@xxx.com

Job Objective

A professional position in engineering safety with a local government agency, with an emphasis on fire protection.

Education

Bachelor of Science in Chemical Engineering.
University of Illinois, Chicago, 2003.
GPA 3.86.
Minor in Fire Protection Engineering.
Major course work included structures chemistry, chemical engineering, fire protection engineering, thermodynamics, hydrology, and electromagnetics.

Experience

Intern, Oakwood Fire Department, Oakwood, Illinois, Summer 2003.
- Employed full-time as assistant to the fire chief. Underwent rigorous three-week training in fire fighting, prevention, and protection.
- Participated in site clearances and arson investigations. Proposed new procedures for responding to college dormitory fire alarms, which resulted in a 25 percent quicker response time.

Assistant Safety Technician, University of Illinois Public Health and Safety Department, Fall 2002 to Winter 2003.
- Worked part-time providing on-site training in public health and safety issues.
- Worked with safety specialists in fire, electrical, chemical, and nuclear emergency preparedness. Trained in recognizing potential fire, health, and safety hazards.

Residential Adviser, University of Illinois Student Housing Department, Fall 2001 to Spring 2002.
- Supervised residential hall wing that housed 75 students.
- Responsible for safety surveillance, counseling, and coordinating building maintenance.

References

Available upon request.

TERRANCE W. WICKSTROM

230 S.E. First Avenue

White Beach, Florida 33128

(407) 555-0036

terrancewickstrom@xxx.com

SUMMARY OF QUALIFICATIONS

Certified Professional Engineer. Twelve years of experience in engineering plus extensive experience in the design and installation of subterranean pipe systems, including layout design, routing, and isometric drawings for pipe spooling. Engineering design experience includes equipment support structures, equipment, and pipe supports. Extensive field experience with both large industrial and civil projects.

EDUCATION AND TRAINING

Bachelor of Science Degree, Engineering, University of Florida, Tampa, 1999.
    Engineering Coursework: Fluids, Mechanics, Stress Analysis, Hydrology, Stress Dynamics, Thermodynamics, Water Treatment Engineering.

Associate of Science Degree, Engineering Specialty, College of Technology, Miami, 1992.
    Completed Engineering Technician training.

EMPLOYMENT HISTORY

Savenant & Ward, Construction Engineering
One S.W. Vermilion, Tampa, Florida
1996 to Present

- Responsible for checking piping systems for proper construction against piping specifications and contact drawings.
- Checked fitting, welding, material class, and support structures.
- Conducted hydro testing of the systems and bolt torquing, according to specifications.
- Worked on the Shell Oil Company off-shore drilling project initial design phase.

EMPLOYMENT HISTORY (continued)

J. L. Winterman and Associates, AIA, Architecture
126 Minter Avenue, Tampa, Florida
1991 to 1996

- Served as engineering technician on large-scale building designs for residential, commercial, industrial, and civil projects.
- Worked closely with structural engineers and city planners to design optimum installation plans for water and sewage pipe placement, routing, and support.
- Designed more efficient pipe support systems, now considered standard for multi-story structures in the Tampa area.

MEMBERSHIPS

National Society of Professional Engineers (NSPE)
Florida Society of Professional Engineers (FSPE)
National Society of Black Engineers

REFERENCES ON REQUEST

Martle Johnson

P.O. Box 17384, Salt Lake City, UT 84132
(801) 555-2757
martlejohnson@xxx.com

Objective

A position as field engineer with a large Northwest utility company, involving expertise in quality assurance, safety, and inspection.

Experience

Bechtel Power Corporation, Salt Lake City / January 2001 to present.
Field Engineer: Perform quality assurance inspections to comply with ASME codes in the installation of embedded and exposed piping of large diameter, sizing of structural components for supports, and checking of structural drawings and specifications.

Western Power Corporation, Salt Lake City / May 1996 to December 2000.
Designer and Field Engineer: Designed oil refinery piping systems. Inspected construction site and tested for stress, hydrology, and support. Performed stress analysis on plates, bolts, and structural steel.

Sundance International Corp., Salt Lake City / June 1991 to May 1996.
Designer and Checker: Checked design drawings for dimensional correctness, pipe size. Rendered layout and elevation drawings for construction projects. Provided on-site checking of "as built" drawings.

Mid-State Kiln Inc., Salt Lake City / June 1989 to June 1991.
Checker: Involved with checking equipment drawings for dimensional correctness and to determine the feasibility of constructing equipment as designed.

Education

Associate Degree in General Engineering, 1989.
Utah College of Technology, Salt Lake City.

U.S. Air Force, 1986 to 1989.
Engineering crew of aircraft carrier, two years.

References

Provided upon request.

SARALYNNE KVITKA

654 S.W. Marshall Street • Jackson, Mississippi 39215
(601) 555-4932 • saralynne@xxx.com

EDUCATION

Bachelor of Architecture, with a minor in Environmental Studies
University of Mississippi, March 2003
Areas of Emphasis:
Structures, Geology, Geography
Environmental Control Systems
Public Planning, Policy, and Management

Jackson Community College, August 1999
AutoCAD, Release 12, AutoDesk Training Center

EXPERIENCE

Engineering Specialist
State of Mississippi, Engineering Division, Jackson
(April 2003 to present)
Proofread, compile, and distribute specifications. Design files for drawing storage and
organize current system. Conduct drawing research for various projects. Create database files for several Port accounts.

Engineering Intern
State of Mississippi, Engineering Division, Jackson
(June 2002 to September 2002, December 2002)
Prepared and submitted permit applications. Received, processed, and distributed
requests for utility locales. Updated house addressing maps for all facilities. Organized
microfilm for all drawings from 1891 to 1995.

Draftsperson
Smithson, Davis & Forbes, Architects, Jackson, Mississippi
(January 2002 to March 2002)
Drafted preliminary through construction drawings. Researched building codes and product information. Practicum experience for academic credit.

ADDITIONAL SKILLS

Intermediate skills and experience with IBM software, including AutoCAD, Paradox, MS
DOS, MS Windows, MS Word, Excel, and Lotus Notes
Some Macintosh experience including MS Word
Art media, model making, and photography

REFERENCES

Available on request

JOAN D. WILHITE

445 S. Alameda • Flagstaff, AZ 86024
(602) 555-3476 • joanwilhite@xxx.com

PROFESSIONAL OBJECTIVE

Chemical engineering position with supervisory and quality control responsibilities

PROFESSIONAL EXPERIENCE

GEOTECHNICAL SPECIALTIES, INC., FLAGSTAFF, AZ
Production Engineering Coordinator (2004–Present)
- Monitor production and controlling quality
- Troubleshoot production problems
- Supervise and motivate 21 technicians
- Create daily production and downtime reports using MS Excel
- Work with chief engineers on production problem resolution
- Lead meetings, review production and safety data
- Using Quality Analyst 4.2, produce capability studies and control charts
- Interact with Accounting, Quality Control, and Personnel on maximization of production line operation
- Best-running production line in the facility (out of five)

Engineering-Technician (2002–2004)
- Successfully performed chemical analysis on finished product (moisture analysis with Technicon/vacuum ovens; sodium analysis with atomic absorption using Perkin Elmer 3100; and ph/salt/titratable acidity)
- Finished product surveys and sensory evaluations
- Maintained process data on Quality Analyst 4.2
- Assisted production coordinators on quality parameters to reduce potential problems
- Set up statistical sampling plans for held product
- Trained management and union representatives on Statistical Methods for Improving Performance

NEWVISION INDUSTRIES, INC., PHOENIX, AZ
Quality Assurance Chemist (2000–2002)
- Analyzed raw ingredients/finished products/environmental swabs
- Conducted Good Manufacturing Practices (GMP) inspections and suggested corrective measures where necessary

NEWVISION INDUSTRIES (continued)
• Interacted with Sanitation Foreman on updating and implementing standardized cleaning procedures
• Wrote/revised procedures manual
• Ordered Micro Laboratory supplies
• Increased volume of testing, which resulted in improved troubleshooting and problem resolution

EDUCATIONAL BACKGROUND

B.S. Degree in Chemical Engineering (March 2000)
University of Washington, Seattle, WA

Continuing Education Seminars:
• How to Organize & Manage Priorities (National Seminars Group)
• Applications in the Management of Quality (Arizona Institute of Technology)
• Certified Quality Technician [#7484] (American Society for Quality Control)
• Statistical Methods for Improving Performance (Nabisco Food Groups)
• Applied Statistical Quality Control Seminar (Northwest Analytical, Inc.)
• Cultivating Supervisory Skills (Portland Community College)
• Successful Communications Skills (Fred Pryor Seminar)
• How to Work with Difficult People (National Seminars Group)

ACTIVITIES/MEMBERSHIPS

• American Society of Quality Control (Arizona Chapter 1043)
• American Society of Chemical Engineers (Arizona/University of Washington chapters)
• Presented paper on pilot plant processing at ASCE conference, 2003, Washington, D.C.

References available upon request

RUSSELL WHITE

6225 Burlington Road   Russell-White@xxx.com
Sioux Falls, SD 57106   Home (605) 555-1212
                                                        Work (605) 555-1983

EDUCATION

South Dakota State University, Brookings, SD
Bachelor of Science, May 1999

Majors: Electrical Engineering, Engineering Physics
Minor: Mathematics
Cumulative GPA: 3.7/4.0, 167 credits

Technical Electives: Microprocessors, Optical Fiber Communication, Biomedical
Instrumentation, Energy Conversion, Statistics, Programming in C++,
FORTRAN, Financial Management, Accounting I & II

WORK EXPERIENCE

Raven Industries, Sioux Falls, SD (May 1999–present)
Engineering Responsibilities:
• Design open and closed loop flow control systems using INTEL 8051 micro
  controller and "C++" programming language.
• Develop new sensors for use with control systems.
• Manage and coordinate activities between engineering, sales, drafting, pur-
  chasing, and production departments.
• Responsible for writing operating manuals and test procedures for each control
  system designed.
• Successfully completed control systems for use in agricultural spraying and
  transplanting, winter highway maintenance, and road construction.
• Responsible for project success from initial design through production.
• Work closely with customers to design control systems to meet their needs.

Other Responsibilities:
• Actively participate on a committee to implement TQM.
• Helped plan the United Way fund-raising drive.

Page 1 of 2

WORK EXPERIENCE *(continued)*

Southwestern Company, Nashville, TN
Student manager (1995–1997)
• Recruited, trained, managed, and motivated college students for summer work in direct sales of educational reference books.
• Received 30 hours sales management training each summer.
• Increased 1995 personal production 56 percent over previous year.

Sales Representative (summers, 1995–1997)
• Independent contractor in direct sales.
• Averaged $13,000 in sales each summer.
• Received 60 hours direct sales training yearly.

Awards received
• Gold Seal Gold Award (worked 80+ hours each week of summer)
• Century Club (top 15 percent of sales force)

ACTIVITIES

• Institute of Electrical and Electronics Engineers
• National Society of Professional Engineers College
• Student Association Senate
• Farm House Fraternity--Treasurer ($100,000 budget), Executive Council
• Joint Engineering Council
• Chairman of South Dakota Inventor's Congress planning committee

References provided on request.

Jeffrey J. Gisler   12847 W. Hudson Street
Peoria, Illinois 61604
(309) 555-0987
jeffgisler@xxx.com

Objective: To obtain a challenging position as a senior-level development or design engineer in a progressive company with a potential for growth.

Education: Bradley University, Masters of Business Administration, May 2004.
GPA: 4.0/4.0

Purdue University, Masters of Science in Mechanical Engineering, May 2000.
Thesis Topic: Effervescent Atomization at Low-Air Liquid Ratios.
GPA: 3.9/4.0, Cum Laude

University of Illinois at Urbana-Champaign, Bachelor of Science in Mechanical Engineering, May 1998.
GPA: 4.7/5.0, Cum Laude

Work Experience: Caterpillar, Inc., Peoria, Illinois, Test Engineer, Technical Services Division, January 2000 to Present
• Worldwide responsibility for all testing and development of purchased hydraulic pumps and motors.
• Lead test/development engineer for proprietary track-loader travel motor.
• Member of ISO 9002 Quality System Implementation Team.

Purdue University, West Lafayette, Indiana
Research Assistant, August 1999 to December 1999
• Developed an environmentally safe nozzle for consumer product spray application.
• Assisted in spray combustion research project.

Publications: Jeffrey J. Gisler, Larry Olson, and David White, "Entrainment by Ligament-Controlled Effervescent Atomizer-Produced Sprays," *Int. J. Multiphase Flow*, 23 (5) pp. 856–884, July 2001.

Publications *(cont'd)*:   Jeffrey J. Gisler, Larry Olson, and David White, "Ligament-Controlled Effervescent Atomization," *Atomization & Sprays*, 7 (4) pp. 383–406, July–August 1997.

Jeffrey J. Gisler, Larry Olson, and David White, "Reducing Solvent and Propellant Emissions from Consumer Productions," Air & Waste Management Association and U.S. EPA International Symposium on Engineering Solution to Indoor Air Quality Problems, Raleigh, North Carolina, July 21–23, 2001.

Honors & Activities: • Community NOW!
• Christmas in April
• Pi Tau Sigma National Mechanical Engineering Society
• Tau Beta Pi National Engineering Honor Society
• Dean's List, 1996–1998

References: Available on request

RASHAD AHMED

1287 NW Vine Avenue • Jonesboro, Arkansas 72403
Cell: (501) 555-9846 • Email: rashadahmed@xxx.com

OBJECTIVE

To work with a major engineering specialty firm in the development of new start-up enterprises.

PROFESSIONAL EXPERIENCE

January 2001 to present
VARITECH
Jonesboro, Arkansas   Position: Director

> Developed a new business, which includes managing the engineering, development, design, production, and marketing of a new product in the field of personal protection for women. The product was tremendously successful and marketed internationally.

February 1997 to December 2001
TURBOMAG CORPORATION
Dallas, Texas   Position: Director

> Secured funds for venture capital from private sources in order to initiate the start of an energy research firm under the direction of the Technical Education Department (TED Center), Ft. Worth Community College. Upon receipt of the initial funds, I developed and managed the project as director and engineer. I was responsible for effective time and financial management, clear and precise project direction, research coordination, experimental results, consultant activity, machine shop fabrication, and working models.

July 1993 to February 1997
SOUTHWEST PIPELINE CORPORATION
Jonesboro, Arkansas   Position: Project contractor

> Developed property and subdivisions and remodeled homes as a sideline, including land clearing, street construction, building, and utility installation as contractor. Emphasis on utility and road construction.

EDUCATION

Edison Technical Institute
Dallas, Texas
B.S., Electrical Engineering, 1993

Automation Institute
Little Rock, Arkansas
Electrical Engineering Technology Certificate, 2000

References available on request.

✣ Donna Everson ✣

1233 Mission Street ✣ San Pablo, California 98329
(213) 555-0812 ✣ donnaeverson@xxx.com

✣ Goal

An engineering management position requiring analysis and
strategic planning.

✣ Education

Massachusetts Institute of Technology, 1990, M.S., Civil Engineering
University of California, Los Angeles, 1988, B.S., Engineering

✣ Experience

CH2M Hill Inc., Civil Engineer, 2001–present
- ✣ Responsible for analysis and design of transportation systems.
- ✣ Coordinated planning and construction with city, state, and federal
  government engineers.
- ✣ Successfully negotiated contract for $26.8 million in highway construc-
  tion for the city of Los Angeles.
- ✣ Responsible for developing cost-benefit ratios, staff and material
  estimates and schedules, and project budgets.
- ✣ Experienced with computer-aided design, drafting, and structural
  analysis.

Shell Oil Company, Engineering Sales Specialist, 1991–2000
- ✣ Responsible for home heating oil sales program and technical support
  for distribution companies.
- ✣ Designed and implemented a marketing program for potential distributors that resulted in 23 percent increased sales over the previous
  year.
- ✣ Developed a network of technical support for both distributors and
  end-users of the product.
- ✣ Coordinated marketing and sales programs with heater manufacturers
  to stimulate sales in the small business market.

✣ Honors

- ✣ Michaelson-Davis Award for Outstanding Contribution from a New
  Employee, 2002
- ✣ Who's Who in Engineering, 2000
- ✣ Chapter President, Society of Women Engineers, 1999–2001
- ✣ Phi Kappa Phi
- ✣ Delta Upsilon Pi, Engineering Honorary

References available on request.

Aaron Wilson

224 Jubilee Road
Indianapolis, IN 46227
(317) 555-2753
aaronwilson@xxx.com

Summary

Seven years of experience in Manufacturing Engineering and Quality Assurance. Major strengths include the ability to manage multiple projects, solve problems, train others, and organize. A dedicated, dependable, flexible, and independent individual with excellent communication and leadership skills.

Education

Bachelor of Science Degree, Computer Integrated Manufacturing Technology Purdue University, West Lafayette, IN, May 1998

Professional Experience

NSK Corporation, Franklin, IN
Precision Ball Screw Manufacturing Plant
(8/99 to Present)

Quality Assurance Assistant Manager (3/04 to Present)
Engineer in Charge of Quality Assurance (11/02 to 3/04)

- Manage department of one engineer and six team members.
- Develop and monitor $400,000 annual budget.
- Coordinate recurrence prevention activities for both internal and external quality problems.
- In charge of ISO 9002 implementation.
- Evaluate "New Business" projects and quote special projects and prototypes.
- Develop and evaluate suppliers.
- Communicate effectively with customers, corporate quality assurance, and other departments regarding quality issues.

Professional Experience (continued)

Manufacturing Engineer--Heat Treatment/Pre-Heat Treatment
(5/01 to 10/02)

- Spent three months training in Maebashi, Japan (5/01 to 7/01).
- Installed and started up $1.3 million induction hardening machine.
- Wrote standard procedures for operation, inspection, and maintenance for heat treatment and pre-heat treatment processes.
- Trained all heat treatment and pre-heat treatment operators.
- Analyzed and improved quality and productivity in the processes.
- Installed and started up CNC lathe for pre-heat treatment turning.
- Sourced, installed, and started up NC band saw.
- Developed and brought online an outside heat treatment source for carburizing.

Manufacturing Engineer--Quality Assurance (8/99 to 4/01)

- Spent three months training in Maebashi, Japan (9/99 to 11/99).
- Installed and started up all plant inspection processes.
- Wrote procedures for operation, inspection, and maintenance for all inspection processes.

References on request.

CHEN WA CHANG

22 S. Gordon Avenue
Dallas, Texas 75232
(214) 555-4459
cwchang@xxx.com

MAJOR EMPLOYMENT AND ACCOMPLISHMENTS

March 1998 to present
ITT Communications, Houston, Texas
Position: District Manager

> Served as manager responsible for the nine area counties for engineering and service. Prepared a budget and sales forecast for the service shop and sales staff; directed support and overhead costs, revenue projections, personnel management, sales and service programs, public relations, and mountaintop site development and management; employed the pinpoint marketing technique I developed at CBG Electronics.

September 1993 to February 1998
CBG Electronics Division, Dallas, Texas
Position: Service Manager/Marketing Manager

> Responsible for management of servicing and maintenance, mountaintop site development, frequency coordination, customer relations for system changes, and marketing. As marketing manager, designed a pinpoint marketing approach to sales efforts based on a study of market trends and license application histories that proved extremely effective; promoted this practice within the firm's sales and service personnel.

July 1986 to August 1993
Southwest Communications, Dallas/Ft. Worth/Houston, Texas
Position: Sales Engineer

> Managed sales activity for Southwest as well as being regional manufacturer representative for organizations and service shops around twelve southwest and south-central states. Served as sales engineer, designing and promoting radiotelephone systems to all types of business and governmental agencies, such as rural fire and police protection agencies. Responsible for developing several mountaintop communication sites, power transmission lines, tower design and construction, access roads, pipelines, and generator facilities.

Page 1 of 2

MAJOR EMPLOYMENT AND ACCOMPLISHMENTS *(continued)*

September 1983 to June 1986
Seeds, Inc., Dallas, Texas
Position: Legislative Liaison
Responsible for lobbying, addressing, and monitoring all proposed legislation for start-up seed money for small businesses as part of the State Economic Development Bill.

EDUCATION

Southern Methodist University, Dallas, Texas
Ph.D., Applied Electronics, 1987
Additional course work in business administration and marketing.

Southern Methodist University, Dallas, Texas
B.S., Communications Engineering, 1977

MILITARY SERVICE

U.S. Army Corps of Engineers, 1971 to 1974
Instructor: heavy equipment operation, maintenance, and safety.

PROFESSIONAL ORGANIZATIONS

• Institute of Electrical and Electronic Engineers
• American Physical Society
• Society for Technical Communication

EXTENDED EDUCATION

• Sales Motivation ITT, Reno, Nevada
• Sales Management ITT, Lynchburg, Virginia
• Motivating People ITT, Portland, Oregon
• Time Management ITT, Miami, Florida
• Working With Government Southwestern Region Conference, IEEE, Phoenix, Arizona
• Business Planning Pryor Seminars, Dallas, Texas
• Technical Writing Southwestern Region Conference, IEEE, Dallas, Texas

REFERENCES

Available upon request.

Gregory G. Gaines

P.O. Box 234 • Saginaw, MI 48603 • (517) 555-4438 • gregorygaines@xxx.com

Experience Summary

More than seven years of varied hydrogeologic experience in performing and managing remedial investigations and assessments. Project responsibilities include design, implementation, and management of site investigation programs and personnel, subcontractor coordination, budget tracking, report preparation, and interaction with regulatory agencies.

Education

M.S., Geology, Oregon State University, Corvallis, OR, 1996.
With strong emphasis in engineering technology.

B.A., Geology, Shawnee State University, Portsmouth, OH, 1994.

Work History

Senior Engineer, Schmidt-Havens Engineering Corporation, Saginaw, MI.
July 2004 to present. (Previous positions held include: Engineer, Senior Geologist, Engineering Specialist, 1996 to 2004.)

Key projects include:
- Field team leader in charge of a remedial investigation (RI) at an NPL Superfund site in Detroit, MI. Responsible for implementing and managing the following field programs: surface water/sediment sampling, soil sampling, drilling, groundwater sampling, packer tests, air sampling, and residential well sampling. Also responsible for RI report.
- Field team leader in charge of drilling and monitoring of well installation at various sites for the Michigan Department of Transportation.
- Supervised drilling and monitoring of well installation at various oil and gas terminals and service stations throughout northern Michigan as part of a property transfer.
- Supervised a hydrogeologic investigation, including drilling, monitoring well installation, and soil and groundwater sampling, at a major steel manufacturing facility in Pennsylvania. Responsible for field investigation reports.

Professional Affiliations

- AIPG Certified Professional Geologist
- Registered Professional Geologist, Michigan, Minnesota, Pennsylvania, Ohio, Indiana, Illinois, Iowa, New York
- Certified Engineering Technician

References, registration numbers, and certificates also available.

CHARLES ANDAWA

4783 West Maple • Baltimore, MD 021233 • (301) 555-2983 • c.andawa@xxx.com

OBJECTIVE:

A position in chemical engineering with a federal agency

EXPERIENCE:

Senior Project Manager, PPD, Inc., Baltimore, MD, 1998-present

- Report to senior vice president of engineering. Supervise 32 employees.
- Direct, supervise, administer, and manage several projects from inception to start-up, including new chemical process equipment manufacturing.
- Assist Sales Department in reviewing the system process design, scheduling, engineering, and costs before final proposal is presented to client.
- Conceived, initiated, and developed chemical formations for non-toxic solutions for use in oil recovery and recycling.
- Formulated empirical equations and design criteria for the system, which resulted in increasing company sales sevenfold over the last five years.
- Instituted procedures for project document handling, filing, and project communication, including project status summaries to management and clients.
- Trained project engineers and project managers to design and manage projects.
- Participated in developing service-system study concept to introduce PPD's name into new markets, which increased sales by 50 percent in that market.

Senior Project and Process Engineer, Moreland Chemical, Annapolis, MD, 1990-1998

- Project experience included Pulp Liquor Evaporation System operations, sand reclamation systems, waste wood utilization to manufacture charcoal, sewage sludge oxidation, waste oxidation, and heat recovery.
- Responsible for planning, scheduling, process design, and specifications.
- Held complete process and project responsibility of four projects from proposal stage through plant start-up, including budgeting.
- Supervised 23 chemical and physical engineers and laboratory technicians.

Process and Plant Engineer, Cecero's, Inc., Annapolis, MD, 1988-1990

- Major responsibilities included chemical plant troubleshooting; process studies; process development; project cost estimation; equipment design; equipment sizing, selection, and purchasing; utility optimization; air and water pollution controls; boiler and incinerator operations; and coordination of plant work with production department.

Process Development Engineer, U.S. Chemical Co., Philadelphia, PA, 1985-1988

- Worked on a solvent exchange and through-air drying of tissue paper.
- Operated the high-speed pacer machine to test the through-air drying concept.

EDUCATION:

M.S., Chemical Engineering, 1985
Minnesota Technical University, Houghton, MN

References: available by request

JEFFERSON BIRD

3829 HIGH ROAD • WARWICK, RI 02887

(401) 555-9287 • jeffersonbird@xxx.com

OBJECTIVE

A position in engineering management in the public sector.

SUMMARY

More than twenty years of experience in construction and mechanical engineering for private corporations, specifically: field engineer for installation of propulsion turbine plant on land-based test site; industrial and product engineering in the shipbuilding, material handling, chemical, and gas industries in construction, maintenance, engineering, and administrative capacities.

EDUCATION

M.S., Mechanical Engineering, 1985
Eastern University, Springfield, MA

B.S., Mechanical Engineering, 1981
Pennsylvania Institute of Technology, Pittsburgh, PA

EXPERIENCE

1995–2002
Newport Shipbuilders, Inc., Warwick, RI, Senior Engineer
• Supported construction and operating personnel during installation, start-up, and testing of propulsion, generator, and hydraulic machinery.
• Performed facility survey, prepared technical reports, and provided engineering support during construction, start-up, and testing of the propulsion turbine plant.
• Assisted in construction during structural and mechanical equipment support and foundation.
• Coordinated fabrication and installation of full size mock-up for integrated sub-base turbo generator.
• Provided support to designers, draftsmen, and construction personnel to ensure compliance with technical specifications and code requirements.

EXPERIENCE *(continued)*

1990–1994
Shipbuilders Corporation, Providence, RI, Engineering Supervisor
- Designed various mechanical and fluid systems and assisted in procurement, installation, and testing of systems and equipment.
- Designed and assisted in construction and testing of a flow-through crude oil handling system on 120,000-ton double-hull tanker, reducing initial cost and increasing operational efficiency.
- Organized a multidisciplinary team to develop and build an oil-water separator to meet pollution control requirements.
- Conducted equipment and system test at the factory and after completion of installation for various components, including pumps, heat exchangers, hydraulics, and control/monitoring devices.
- Assisted in installation and testing of bulk petrochemical heating system to maintain the product temperature.

1985–1989
TEC, Fiber Division, Boston, MA, Staff Engineer
- Assisted during installation, start-up, and testing of machinery for fiber, film cellulose, and bulk material and processing equipment.
- Developed and assisted in installation of automated overhead conveying system to replace manual material handling operation for cellulose sheet.
- Supervised installation of the filling line to increase bagging output for micro crystalline cellulose.
- Redesigned the PVC blown film machine and provided assistance during installation and start-up.

1981–1984
Pennsylvania Oxygen Corp., Ltd., Pittsburgh, PA, Assistant Engineer
- Supervised a workforce of 120 with responsibility over production and maintenance of oxygen and acetylene plant and facilities.
- Conducted the economic analysis for relocating oxygen plant. Supervised erection of the plant at the new site.
- Designed and assisted in the fabrication of the filtering system for acetylene. Supervised start-up and the testing of the system.
- Developed the test procedure for high-pressure cylinders to meet regulatory requirements.

REFERENCES ON REQUEST

• KEVIN FOXWORTH •

2114 Renton Street • Kirkland, Washington 98005
(206) 555-3497 • kfoxworth@xxx.com

• CAREER OBJECTIVE

Engineering position with an industrial manufacturing company.

• EDUCATION

B.S., Engineering, University of Washington, 1999

A.A., Technology & Industry Production, Everett Community College, Everett, Washington, 1989

• CAPABILITIES

- Manage continuous fire furnaces that produce flat pressed glass and glass for machine and hand blowing.
- Plan and supervise all aspects of furnace operation and maintenance, including personnel scheduling and staffing.
- Evaluate alternative production methods and materials to reduce costs and improve product quality.
- Control raw materials inventory, ordering, and inspection.
- Train employees in use and maintenance of equipment.
- Review product availability and equipment developments to keep systems up-to-date for both production and safety concerns.
- Plan, coordinate, and supervise all aspects of glassware production.

• ACHIEVEMENTS

- Initiated improved method for raw materials handling that resulted in $250,000 in actual savings.
- Worked with production engineers to develop new heating procedures that made furnaces 20 percent more efficient in start-up time.
- Developed operating procedures that improved worker safety.
- Designed alternative casing that reduced external temperatures dramatically, thus decreasing fire and burn hazard.
- Given Award of Merit for developing material composition that produced greater clarity in pressed glass products.

• WORK HISTORY

Pilchuck GlassWorks Factory, Seattle, Washington, 1991–present
Furnace/Production Manager

Boeing, Renton, Washington, 1989–1991
Senior Technician, Instrumentation Casing Section

• REFERENCES

Available when requested.

STEPHEN MONETTI
34 South Avon Street
Charleston, South Carolina 29411
(603) 555-2236
stephenmonetti@xxx.com

CAREER ACHIEVEMENTS AND RESPONSIBILITIES
- Direct, supervise, and administer turn-key projects from inception to start-up for equipment manufacturing firm.
- Coordinate with sales department to review system process design, equipment sizes, schedule, and engineering costs before presenting final proposal to the client.
- Negotiate purchases and advise corporate president and CEO of pending contracts and negotiations.
- Supervise four project management teams, including 12 engineers and 16 draftsmen.
- Completed 17 domestic projects and 20 international projects in Latin America, South America, Spain, and Africa.
- Conceived, initiated, and successfully sold design of two new equipment products that resulted in a 40 percent increase in corporate sales over two years.
- Completed all projects on or ahead of schedule. All projects resulted in corporate profits; many produced higher profits than anticipated.
- Trained project engineers and project managers to design and manage assigned projects.
- Instituted program for college interns and developed training program that culminated in job offers to those graduates whose performance met challenges of the position. After seven years, all students thus hired are still with the company and highly productive.
- Acted as site project engineer during construction of $250 million plant.
- Registered professional engineer in South Carolina and Arkansas.

CAREER EXPERIENCE
- Senior Engineer, DRG Inc., Charleston, South Carolina, 1994–present
- Senior Project and Process Engineer, Hopewell Systems, Charleston, South Carolina, 1990–94
- Consultant Engineer, Toverston Dryers, Little Rock, Arkansas, 1987–90
- Process Development Engineer, James River Corp., Neenah, Wisconsin, 1983–87

EDUCATION
M.S., Chemical Engineering, Georgia Institute of Technology, Atlanta, 1994
B.S., Engineering, University of Wisconsin, Milwaukee, 1993

References available upon request.

DARIUS G. W. HARMS

3485 Plainfield Road
Lincoln, Nebraska 68573
Cell: (402) 555-9287
E-mail: dariusharms@xxx.com

CAREER GOAL

A position in Engineering Management in the public sector

ACHIEVEMENTS & EXPERIENCE

- Supported construction and operating personnel during installation, start-up, and testing of propulsion generator and hydraulic machinery.
- Performed facility survey, prepared technical reports, and provided engineering support during construction, start-up, and testing of the propulsion turbine plant.
- Directed structural and mechanical equipment development and operations.
- Coordinated fabrication and installation of full-size mock-up for integrated sub-base turbo generator.
- Provided support to designers, draftsmen, and construction personnel to ensure compliance with technical specifications and code requirements.
- Designed various mechanical and fluid systems and assisted in procurement, installation, and testing of systems and equipment.
- Designed and assisted in construction and testing of a flow-through crude oil handling system on oil recycler, reducing initial cost and increasing operational efficiency.
- Conducted equipment and system test at the factory and after site installation of various recycling components, including pumps, heat exchangers, hydraulics, and control/monitoring devices.
- Aided in installation and testing of bulk petrochemical heating system.
- Assisted during installation, start-up, and testing of machinery for fiber, film cellulose, bulk material, and processing equipment.
- Developed and assisted in installation of automated overhead conveying system to replace manual material-handling operation for cellulose sheet.

PAGE 1 OF 2

- Supervised installation of the filling line to increase bagging output for micro crystalline cellulose.
- Redesigned the PVC blown film machine and provided support during installation and start-up.
- Supervised a workforce of 120 with responsibility over production and maintenance of oxygen and acetylene plant and facilities.
- Conducted the economic analysis for relocating oxygen plant.
- Oversaw erection of the plant at the new site.
- Designed and supported in the fabrication of the filtering system for acetylene.
- Supervised start-up and the testing of the system.
- Developed the test procedure for high-pressure cylinders to meet regulatory requirements.

WORK HISTORY

Senior Engineer, 1999–2004
Benton Recycling Machinery, Inc., Lincoln, Nebraska

Engineering Supervisor, 1990–1999
Taber Manufacturing, Lincoln, Nebraska

Staff Engineer, Maintenance Engineer, Technician, 1981–1990
Tutwiller Bond Oxygen Corp., Ltd., Topeka, Kansas

EDUCATION

M.S., Mechanical Engineering, 1987
University of Kansas

B.S., Mechanical Engineering, 1981
University of Nebraska-Lincoln

References on request

Bruce Cox, Jr.
Marine Systems Engineer

Present Address:
P.O. Box 601   6225 Edison Drive
United States Merchant Marine Academy
Reading, PA 19605
brucecox@xxx.com
(516) 555-5622

Education:
United States Merchant Marine Academy
Bachelor of Science, June 1999
Major: Marine Systems Engineering (ABET Accredited)

License:
USCG Certified Third Assistant Engineer for Steam and Diesel, Unlimited
Tonnage

Certifications:
USCG Lifeboatman, Marine Firefighting, Hazardous Materials Training, Red
Cross CPR and Emergency Medical Procedures

Computer Skills:
Word Processing (Word, Works), Spreadsheets (Quattro Pro, Excel, TK Solver,
Access), Drafting (AutoCad, Cadkey), Programming (Basic, C++, COBOL)

Career-Related Experiences:
Sailed as Engine Cadet aboard the following vessels:
- SS *Northern Lights*
      Totem Ocean Trailer Express
- MV *Sea-Land Voyager*
      Sea-Land Services, Inc.
- SS *Kainalu*
      Matson Navigation Company
- SS D*enali*
      Keystone Shipping Company
- MV *Sea-Land Explorer*
      Sea-Land Services, Inc.

Career-Related Experiences: *(continued)*

Completed 300 days of shipboard training as an Engine Cadet. Duties on the ships included watchstanding, maintenance, and daily operation. Also assisted in casualty procedures experienced at sea.

Internship:

Performed an internship at Parsons Power, Wyomissing, PA. Involved in the design process of two gas turbine cogeneration plants. Also assisted in the design of a radiation containment structure.

Extracurricular Activities:

- Regimental Operations Senior Chief Petty Officer
- Served as third in command of all Second Class Midshipmen
- Department Head in charge of planning and organizing all operations of the Regiment of Midshipmen

Member:

- Society of Naval Architects and Marine Engineers
- American Society of Naval Engineers

References Available Upon Request

Serena Pederson

334 Beca Street
Reno, Nevada 89564
(702) 555-0227
serenapederson@xxx.com

Career Goal

Seeking employment as an associate engineer or mechanical drafter with the engineering department of a major civil engineering firm that offers opportunities for challenge and advancement.

Experience and Work History

2/04 to present
Calham Engineering, West Bonnaville, Nevada
Mechanical Drafter
Mechanical drafting and layout of commercial piping and construction, and on-site sketch drawings of general mechanical layouts.

11/02 to 2/04
Interstate Engineering Company, Las Vegas, Nevada
Mechanical Drafter
Mechanical drafting and layout of marine piping, drawings and electrical diagrams, and on-site sketch drawings of piping and electrical. As-built floor plan drawings.

1/01 to 11/02
Northwest Cedar Homes/Lindal Cedar Homes, Seattle, Washington
Architectural Drafter
Drafting and design of presentation floor plans and elevation site plans in accordance with company and client specifications. Consulting with clients on custom home designs and site plans. Delivery of building materials to job sites.

Education

B.S., Civil Engineering, University of Nevada-Las Vegas, 2004; GPA: 3.5

Extensive classes in architectural drafting from Portland Community College, Portland, Oregon, including: Residential Design; Structural Design; Piping and Electrical Design; AutoCAD; Building Codes

Associate of Applied Sciences Degree (Criminal Justice), Portland Community College, Portland, Oregon, 1995

References on Request

- # JORGE S. HERNANDEZ

  P.O. Box 4432 • Las Cruces, New Mexico 88011 • 505-555-0375
  jorgehernandez@xxx.com

- # OBJECTIVE

  A career track in environmental engineering with a large private or public agency.

- # WORK EXPERIENCE

  Environmental Engineer, 8/02 to present
  Brigante & Solo, Inc., Las Cruces, New Mexico
  Prepare environmental assessments and checklists, noise level predictions, ambient noise levels. Advise design engineering on environmental problems, design cross sections, estimate construction quantities. Compute wetland involvement.

  Utilities Relocation Engineer, 7/00 to 8/02
  Arizona State Department of Transportation, Phoenix, Arizona
  Work with public utilities in relocation of facilities within public right of way. Coordinate movement and develop movement agreements. Enforce clear zone.

  Engineer, 6/99 to 7/00
  Arizona State Department of Transportation, Phoenix, Arizona
  Coordinate, review, revise, and process U.S. Army Corps of Engineer permits, shorelines, flood plains, and hydraulic permits. Prepare environmental checklists, impact statements, noise level predictions, ambient noise levels, and air pollution levels. Investigate and advise for hazardous material spills, underground storage tanks, and site assessments. Prepare displays for public and court meetings.

    Review environmental documents and permits, interpret noise levels on projects, design noise barrier, and monitor and collect air quality samples. Review and approve large lots, short plats, and roadway approaches for private developers. Assemble and calibrate nine air quality control sets valued at $175,000 each.

- # EDUCATION

  B.S., Engineering, University of New Mexico, 1999
  3.8 GPA, Cum Laude.

  References will be provided on request.

Brooke Smith

935 Heatherstone Place, Apt. 819, Peoria, IL 61614
(309) 555-1983, E-mail: brookesmith@xxx.com

Education
United States Merchant Marine Academy
Degree: Bachelor of Science, June 2003
Major: Marine Engineering Management
Class Standing: 3.60 of 4.0 (second in class)

USCG License: Third Assistant Engineer, Steam or Diesel, Unlimited Horsepower
Commission: Ensign, United States Naval Reserve, June 2003

Certificates: Advanced Lifesaving/First Aid, Red Cross CPR, USCG Lifeboatman,
Advanced Firefighting

Computer Skills: Word Processing (WordPro, Works), Programming (True Basic),
Cadkey, Spreadsheets (Excel, Works), Project Scheduling Programs (Primavera),
Internet, Netscape Composer, Freelance Graphics, Lotus Notes

Work Experience
Repair Process Engineer
Caterpillar Inc., Peoria, IL

> Member of a self-directed work team developing best practice repair processes
> for a Caterpillar dealership's service department. Contributed to design of the user
> interface for the future service information delivery system. Responsible for cre-
> ating a service operations audit for the 793C wheel station rebuild procedure.
> Develop best practice rebuild standards for Caterpillar components. Attended an
> Applied Failure Analysis class. (July 2003 to present)

Shipboard Training

> Sailed as a Junior Engineering Officer aboard six different U.S. flag vessels. Com-
> pleted a twenty-credit independent study on various shipboard engineering sys-
> tems. Assisted in maintenance and operation aboard both steam and diesel ships.
> (November 2002 to June 2003)

Page 1 of 2

Work Experience (continued)

Industry Internship

Vart, Mathews and Co., Hong Kong

Aided in hull, machinery, and cargo surveys. Assisted during survey of damaged auxiliary engines in Chiwan, P.R.C. Attended joint survey of hull collision with classification society surveyors, admiralty lawyer, and P&I representative. (October 2002)

Leadership Experience

- President of Society of Women Engineers for Kings Point Chapter
- Regimental Alumni Liaison Officer: Worked with senior industry alumni to enhance alumni/midshipmen

Awards

- All-American Scholar Collegiate Award: Selected by dean for outstanding work and academic achievement during college career
- Frank Cashin Award Scholarship for promoting careers in solid waste management and energy production
- Academic Achievement Awards: Dean's list (four years), Sea Year Excellence Ribbon for outstanding performance, Best Electrical Engineering Student

References on request

ROGER W. FENTON

223 S. Cameron Drive • St. Paul, MN 55223
rogerfenton@xxx.com • (612) 555-0443

SUMMARY OF QUALIFICATIONS

Achievement-oriented leader, team player, dedicated to continuous improvement. Diverse experience, including engineering, manufacturing, quality control, customer service, distribution, management, and supervision. Areas of major emphasis include employee and labor relations (extensive background managing in a union shop), machining and assembly, hot extrusion, injection molding, electroplating, safety, budget and forecasting, absentee control, training, and training management.

WORK EXPERIENCE

PLASTIMADE CORP., St. Paul, MN, 2004–Present
(Manufacturer of vinyl products for industrial, government, and consumer markets.)
Production Manager

- Manage 31 employees in all phases of manufacturing, distribution, quality, inventory, and maintenance operations.
- Provided all personnel actions.
- Turned around a troubled manufacturing operation with severe quality and productivity deficiencies in time to support high-demand season sales.
- Eliminated the most costly quality defect--reduced warranty returns to nearly zero.
- Increased production 220 percent.
- Increased average individual productivity by 14 percent.
- Ensured a safe working environment, with no lost-time accidents.

STANLEY INDUSTRIAL TOOLS, Milwaukee, WI, 1996–2004
(Manufacturer of mechanics' hand tools, including sockets and torque wrenches.)
Production Supervisor

- Managed multiple departments, supervised up to 78 employees, responsible for three shifts and continuous operations.
- Planned product, equipment, and manpower to meet production requirements.
- Requisitioned and maintained inventories of tooling and operating supplies.
- Developed and controlled multimillion-dollar department budgets; prepared expense forecasts.
- Maintained a safe, positive, and productive work environment.
- Utilized group technology principles to achieve zero-cost labor operations.
- Reduced product lead times by five weeks, inventory by 20 percent, and customer back orders by 98 percent.
- Managed five product improvement teams (quality circles), implementing modern quality management techniques, i.e., SPC and ISO 9002 international quality standards.
- Realized more than $200,000 in annual savings.

WORK EXPERIENCE *(continued)*
- Developed and implemented "Safety Awareness" program, achieving a lost-time rate 45 percent below the national industry average.
- Developed manufacturing process for 29 models of "industry's best" torque wrenches.
- Modified electroplating system, achieving a 36 percent reduction in process time, a 20 percent reduction in rework, and doubled operational efficiency.
- Managed national product repair center; reduced repair time 63 percent.
- Developed operator training programs and setup procedures for key equipment.

STANLEY INDUSTRIAL TOOLS, Wichita Falls, TX, 1994–1996
Manufacturing Engineer
- Managed start-up operations for the manufacture of torque wrench components.
- Developed and implemented machining methods; established product costs.
- Prepared manufacturing plans and process prints. Designed fixtures and specified tooling.
- Implemented vendor and in-house manufacturing for 387 components, decreasing lead times by 64 days.
- Established a quality program to support manufacturing, reducing scrap and rework by 87 percent.

STANLEY INDUSTRIAL TOOLS, Denver, CO, 1990–1994
Foreman
- Successfully transferred the torque wrench product line to the Colorado plant; increased annual shipments by $4 million.
- Specified and procured state-of-the-art calibration equipment with an accuracy 2.5 times greater than the competitors'.
- Implemented two union wage reclassifications, yielding a labor savings of 11 percent.
- Designed assembly workstations and component storage area to complement each other; reduced material handling by 66 percent.
- Set up and managed component parts inventory valued over $1 million.

EDUCATION
BELLEVUE COMMUNITY COLLEGE, Bellevue, WA
A.S., Electronics Technology, 1990
Coursework: Geometric Dimensioning/Tolerancing; CNC Lathe Programming; CNC Machine Tools (Programming); Heat Treatment of Materials; Engineering Project Management

Additional Training:
- Certificate in Supervisory Training
- Dale Carnegie Management System
- Statistical Process Control (SPC)
- "Just in Time" (JIT) Inventory
- Electroplating and Finishing

REFERENCES ON REQUEST

GEENA MICKELSON

Professional Office Complex 2, Suite 34, Boise, Idaho 83732
(208) 555-3453 • FAX (208) 555-3476
geenamickelson@xxx.com

GENERAL QUALIFICATIONS

I have been a SEPA-NEPA engineer for more than 13 years for Idaho State.

DEPARTMENT OF TRANSPORTATION PROJECTS

- Responsible for assessments, air quality, noise level surveys, permitting, and environmental projects.
- Conducted surveys and projected noise level surveys.
- Wrote major portions of the department's many environmental assessments and 10,000 to 20,000 environmental checklists.
- Determined wetland involvement prior to 1993.
- Coordinated all state, federal, and local permits (according to NEPA and SEPA requirements), and coordinated and negotiated for mitigation.
- Investigated for hazardous waste occurrence.
- For six years screened WSDOT district projects for archaeological and historical significance and contracted for evaluation services.
- Served as the coordinator for District Interdisciplinary Team.
- Seven years' experience as highway engineer for foundation investigation, route survey, geologically sensitive areas; water pollution source investigation and correction; and landslide investigation and correction.

RECENT WORK HISTORY

Senior Transportation Engineer--July 1998 to present
Idaho State Department of Transportation, Boise, Idaho
Inspector on construction projects for new roadways. Test samples and test for quality control. Coordinate contractor schedules. Served as survey party chief for two years.

Transportation Engineer--June 1991 to July 1998
Idaho State Department of Transportation, Boise, Idaho
Test soil samples prior to highway construction and foundation preparation. Make recommendations for quality control, sand equivalent, fine and coarse grade compaction, soil settlement, asphalt extraction, and soil and aggregate mix ratio.

EDUCATION AND TRAINING

University of Idaho, Bachelor of Science (Geology), 1984
University of Idaho, Secondary Certificate (Engineering), 1988
Engineering in the '90s Workshops, 1996, 1999
Effective Report Writing, WSDOT, 1999, 2000
Acoustic Seminar, WSDOT, 1999
Water Quality Research Workshop, 1999
Teletype Operator's Course, 1999
80-Hour Hazardous Waste Handlers Certification, OSHA, EPA, 1999
Noise Highway Traffic and Fundamentals, FHWA, 2001
Miscellaneous Basic Computer Courses, WSDOT, 2002
Underground Storage Tank Removal Certificate, 2002

References available on request.

JOHN B. HANAKA

665 W. Paloma Drive
Tempe, AZ 85275
(602) 555-4439
John-Hanaka@xxx.com

PROFESSIONAL AMBITION
A career in mechanical engineering.

EDUCATION
ARIZONA STATE UNIVERSITY, Tempe, AZ
M.S., 2004, Mechanical Engineering
B.S., 1991, Business, with minor in Industrial Design

QUALIFICATIONS
Master's degree in mechanical engineering. Graduated 12th in a class of 150. Ten years in materials management, operations, and customer service. Ability to analyze and prepare budget forecasts, financial statements, and analytical reports. Proficiency in IBM-36 mainframe and PC. Software applications include AutoCAD, Lotus, Excel, MS Word, Dbase IV, QuattroPro. Supervised, trained, and coordinated group activities.

CONTRACT AND PART-TIME EMPLOYMENT
MACHINE WORKS INDUSTRIES, Tempe, AZ
Purchasing Manager, January–November 2004
• Developed and implemented JIT Materials Management Program for corporate offices and 13 warehouse outlets. Negotiated and purchased three-location, 400-extension telecommunications system. Responsible for $17 million in purchasing. Reported to Finance Director. Contracted to install JIT Materials Management Program. Contract ended at completion of project.

JOHNSON & JOHNSON, Tempe, AZ
Merchandiser, 2001–2003
• Assisted field sales and helped coordinate and set up promotions in retail and trade shows. Part-time position used to finance education. Left in good standing.

Page 1 of 2

PROFESSIONAL EXPERIENCE
DESERT STATES FASTENING SYSTEMS, INC., Tempe, AZ
Buyer/Inventory Control Manager, 1995–2001
- Coordinated day-to-day warehouse operations. Supervised 12 employees.
- Managed inventory control levels and purchasing activities. $20–30 million sales revenue in the fastener industry. Reported to General Manager.
- Corporation relocated to Kent, WA. My commitment to education necessitated the decline of employer's offer to move.

FLEXALLOY, INC., Flagstaff, AZ
Buyer/Warehouse Manager, 1991–1995
- Developed and implemented JIT system reducing inventory levels by 20 percent and reducing freight costs by 50 percent while increasing operating efficiency.
- Reported to Vice President of Operations. Employer downsized; left in good standing.

References available on request.

NAVRONE W. GRIFFITH

17 N.E. THIRD AVENUE
REEDSVILLE, PA 17084-3384
(814) 555-5089
navronegriffith@xxx.com

Career Goal

My career objective is to become an integral part of a progressive,
growth-oriented corporation in the areas of engineering and management.

Education

2004 B.S., Fluid Power Engineering
Milwaukee School of Engineering, Milwaukee, WI
  • Minor taken in Air Conditioning Engineering Technology
  • Journeyman Plumber (PA)
  • Certification for teaching Heating and Air Conditioning (PA)

Career Summary

CASE HOME HEATING AND PLUMBING
1/91 to 9/03 Cincinnati, OH
Part-Owner, Manager, Journeyman Plumber
  Responsible for generating business and assigning workers to complete contracted projects for private, corporate, and civil clients.
  Worked closely with engineering consultants on major plumbing and
  heating installation projects for multistory buildings and large residential complexes. Became part-owner, but sold interest to return to
  college to pursue an engineering career.

Memberships

  • National Society of Black Engineers (president of student chapter at
    MSE)
  • American Society of Heating, Refrigeration and Air Conditioning Engi-
    neers, Inc.
  • American Water Resources Association

References

Available on request.

PAULA R. TREMONE

67 W. Tanner • Concord, NH 03307 • (603) 555-2940 • paulatremone@xxx.com

OBJECTIVE:

A position of responsibility in structural engineering with a civil engineering firm.

SUMMARY OF QUALIFICATIONS:

- Bachelor's degree in structural engineering, graduating with honors.
- Extensive experience in design and construction of commercial and residential structures.
- Reviewed and recommended bids.
- Hired subcontractors.
- Provided on-site supervision of subcontractors.
- Supervised installation of sprinkler systems.
- Construction of offshore oil rigs, mobile home parks, and recreation homes.
- Flat concrete work, electrical, plumbing, and framing.
- Read blueprints and drawings.

EXPERIENCE:

TREMONE AND ASSOCIATES, INC. Concord, NH
Co-Owner/Operator, 1998–2003
Responsible for the day-to-day operation of construction firm as well as consultant for Barker Engineering, Ltd., precision engineering brokers.

BARKER ENGINEERING, LTD. Concord, NH
Manager, 1996–1998
Manager of precision engineering brokerage firm, responsible for hiring, firing, reviewing subcontractors' bids, and negotiating contracts.

RAJ, INC. Santa Cruz, CA
Superintendent, 1993–1996
Engaged in ground-up construction, bank ATM installations, earthquake-proofing of older buildings, and structural steel. Also, general construction of custom homes, apartment buildings, restaurants, remodels, roads and parkways, and a trailer and mobile home park.

EDUCATION:

1999 B.S., Structural Engineering, University of New Hampshire–Durham
1987 A.A.S., Construction Technology, University of California–Santa Cruz

References available on request.

MUHAMMAD SERAW

Home: (802) 555-4312
Cell: (802) 555-4375
2121 W. Hampstead Lane • Rutland, VT 05702 • muhammadseraw@xxx.com

OBJECTIVE   Position in engineering management with the construction
department of a large engineering consulting firm.

EMPLOYMENT   **City of Rutland, Rutland, VT (2000–2004)**
PUBLIC WORKS INSPECTOR II (8/02–3/04)
- Coordinated and performed public works inspections for compliance with project plans, standards, and specifications on projects up to $3 million.
- Ensured that proper materials, methods, and procedures were utilized.
- Interpreted construction requirements for contractors/property owners and assisted in compliance.
- Conducted final inspections and submitted corrections as needed.
- Assisted project civil engineering preparation, revision, and execution of cost estimates, working drawings, change orders, and progress payments.
- Prepared all state and federal on-site records on daily basis.

ENGINEERING TECHNICIAN II (7/00–8/02)
- Coordinated permits and certificates of occupancy.
- Scheduled and coordinated preconstruction meetings with city staff contractors and developers, ensuring that all requirements and conditions for the development were met.
- Arranged engineering inspections and served as liaison between all relevant parties.
- Provided general and technical information concerning city codes, specifications, standards, deeds, easements, utilities, and improvement plans and other related information.
- Processed agreements, bonds, insurance certificates, and other financial provisions for developments.
- Researched and compiled data for monthly and annual reports for city departments and other governmental agencies.

Page 1 of 2

EMPLOYMENT (*continued*)

Sullivan Construction, Waterford, CT (4/98–6/00)
ASSISTANT PROJECT MANAGER
- Consistently came in under budget while responsible for all purchasing and hiring.
- Prepared material take-offs and subcontractor bid packages; purchased construction materials.
- Processed invoices for payment on $20 million multifamily residential projects.
- Reviewed subcontractors' submissions for compliance with architect's and engineers' specifications.
- Reviewed and approved general and subcontractor schedules, conducting weekly job-site meetings to eliminate contractor interference and arranging all local, state, and federal inspections.
- Supervised job-site superintendents, conducting initial field hiring of all general contractor's staff.

Cappers, Inc., Manchester, CT (10/94–4/98)
PURCHASING AGENT
- Purchased construction materials for residential, commercial, and industrial projects of up to $10 million, achieving up to a 75 percent rate of under-budget purchases.
- Assisted in administration of several HUD housing complexes.
- Assembled subcontractor bid packages, received bids, and recommended award of bid.
- Established apprenticeship programs with state trade organizations.

CFD Construction, Inc., Greenwich, RI (5/92–10/94)
ASSISTANT SUPERINTENDENT
- Scheduled material deliveries to sites.
- Prepared certified payrolls.
- Scheduled subcontractors and inspections, and assigned work to general contractor's staff.

EDUCATION

B.S., Engineering and Construction Technology
University of Maine, Farmington, 2000.

A.A.S., Construction and Design
Fort Kent Community College, Maine, 1992.

References upon request.

JASON SWIFT

2216 Marshall Heights Road, Apt. G3
New Orleans, LA 70112
(504) 555-4450
jasonswift@xxx.com

CAREER OBJECTIVE
An entry-level position in Civil Engineering

EDUCATION
Oregon State University, Corvallis, OR
Specialization: Civil Engineering Professional School
Degree: Bachelor of Science in Civil Engineering, expected 12/05

Southern Technical College, New Orleans, LA
Specialization: General Education and Pre-Engineering
Degree: Associate of Science, 12/03
E.I.T. Certificate

COURSE WORK
- Engineering: Statistics, Dynamics, Strength of Materials, and Thermodynamics
- Civil Engineering: Environmental Engineering, Fluid Mechanics, Materials, Soil Mechanics, Structural Design, Surveying, and Transportation

WORK EXPERIENCE
Crew Member, Crowd Management Services, Corvallis, OR
Summers 2004 and 2005

Landscape Subcontractor, Corvallis, OR
Summers 2003 and 2004

ACTIVITIES
- Currently enrolled in certification course for AutoCAD Release 12
- National member of the American Society of Civil Engineers
- A.S.C.E. student chapter vice president
- A.S.C.E. student workshop
- American Institute of Steel Construction bridge design competition, 2004 and 2005
- Sports (baseball, swimming, water polo, basketball, and fishing)
- Woodworking

References available on request

David Riley

234 Bench Street • Denver, CO 80203
David-Riley@xxx.com • (303) 555-9876

Objective

To find a challenging job in one or a combination of the following areas: Test Sales/Service Engineering Support—Research Design. Willing to relocate and travel up to 40 percent of the time.

Education

Bachelor of Science, Mechanical Engineering, University of Denver, CO, 1999
GPA 3.68
Course listing and/or official transcript available upon request

Experience

Caterpillar Corp., Denver, CO, 9/99–present
Product Engineer, 1/04–present
Designed and specified detail parts for systems incorporated in forklift trucks. Variety of systems include electrical, hydraulic, brakes, operator compartment design, and other miscellaneous components required. Included finalization of bill of material listing and drawing clarification.

Maintenance Engineer, 9/02–12/03
Corrected design, manufacturing, or design problems as well as additions of new vendor products of current production lift trucks.

Sales and Products Engineer, 9/99–9/02
Coordinated and provided specifications and technical information to Sales Department for use in sales literature. Extensive use of IBM-compatible personal computers for spreadsheets, basic programming, and word processing.

US Army Corps of Engineers, 1996–1998 (summers)
Hydroelectric Design Branch
Engineering Technician
Calculated preliminary and final performance evaluations on hydraulic turbines for government-owned hydroelectric facilities under supervision of project engineer. Corresponded with different turbine manufacturers for technical data.

References available upon request.

JOANNA CASSIDY

2287 S.W. 29th Place
Savannah, GA 31406
(912) 555-4986
joannacassidy@xxx.com

OBJECTIVE

A Construction Management position with a large engineering firm, utilizing my background and education in construction engineering technology and extensive managerial experience.

EDUCATION

CONSTRUCTION MANAGEMENT: UCLA, Los Angeles, CA
(2000 - 2002)
M.S. Degree, 2002

DESIGN AND CONSTRUCTION ENGINEERING: Austin Peay State
College, Clarksville, TN (1995 - 1999)
B.S. Degree, 1999

CONSTRUCTION ENGINEERING TECHNOLOGY: Middlesex
Community College, Middleton, CT (1992 - 1994)
Certificate: 1994

QUALIFICATIONS

- Public works inspections
- Report preparation
- Expense control/reductions
- Operations/materials management

SKILLS

- Staff hiring/management
- Quality control
- Procurement operations
- Permit procedures

ACHIEVEMENTS

- Consistently brought in construction projects under budget
- Achieved materials procurement rate up to 75 percent under budget
- Instituted apprenticeship program in conjunction with state trade organizations

CERTIFICATION

- PUBLIC WORKS INSPECTOR: UCLA, Los Angeles, CA (2001)
- CONCRETE FIELD TECHNICIAN: American Concrete Institute (1998)
- FITTER: General Dynamics, Electric Boat Division, Apprenticeship (1989)

EMPLOYMENT HISTORY

Jones & Marks, Ltd., Architectural Engineering
Intern (Summer 1998); Part-Time (2002 - Present)
Hired part-time after serving three-month paid internship (selected from among 75 applicants), taking full advantage of on-the-job training in construction design and engineering. Responsible for maintaining blueprints, change notices, design meeting records. Worked with consulting engineers on site preparation, evaluation of design blueprints, and review of construction schedules.

Austin Peay State College, Clarksville, TN
Design Assistant (1996 - 1998)
Worked with faculty on work-for-hire projects from engineering firms and construction contractors. Prepared drawings, conducted stress management calculations, tested other analyses for accuracy.

COMMUNITY SERVICE

- Habitat for Humanity: solicited donations of materials and contractors' crews to build housing for low-income families; provided labor (1999 - 2004)
- Graffiti Abatement Coordinator: solicited donations of materials and coordinated volunteers (2004)
- St. Marks Homeless Shelter Holiday Drive: coordinated city staff volunteers (2002)

REFERENCES AVAILABLE UPON REQUEST

THOMAS CARTER

21 Interstate Street • Portland, Maine 04121 • (207) 555-4335
thomascarter@xxx.com

PROFESSIONAL GOALS

To develop an engineering career with a successful company in the area of machine design, gain a professional engineering certificate, and continue my education.

PROFESSIONAL EXPERIENCE

Project Engineer/Engineering Manager--Sherwin-Williams Paint Company, Portland, Maine
8/04 to present
• Engineering duties include design conception, documentation, and implementation as specified by customer. Act as liaison between engineering and sales departments, from bid to shipment.
• Achievements include introducing two new products into the Sherwin-Williams line.
• Managerial duties include setting engineering documentation policy, distributing workload, and giving input on production schedule and paint operation.

Engineering Assistant--Debenham Manufacturing, Portland, Maine
6/03 to 9/03
• Duties included AutoCAD drafting and hands-on work with prototype machines in the research and development department.

Engineering Assistant--Portland Veterans Hospital
3/99 to 9/00
• Duties included monitoring building HVAC system and metal fabrication.

EDUCATIONAL EXPERIENCE

B.S.M.E., Oregon State University, June 2004
• Achieved a GPA of 3.2/4.0 for classes taken in the professional program.
• Acted as Group Leader for the Computer Controlled Walking Machine Senior Project.

EDUCATIONAL EXPERIENCE *(CONTINUED)*

• Elective course work included Finite Element Analysis, Computer Aided Engineering, Smart Products, and HVAC.

Graduate of Naval Gunnery School as a Rocket Launcher Technician, 1995

MILITARY EXPERIENCE

Gunners Mate Technician--U.S. Navy
3/96 to 3/99
Honorable Discharge
• Duties included operating and maintaining a rocket launcher and gun mount. Handling Supervisor for nuclear and conventional weapons.

REFERENCES

An interview, references, transcripts, and a detailed work history are available upon your request at the above address and phone number.

TAMINA G. RAWLEY

84 S. Banker Street • Santa Clara, CA 95021

(805) 555-4878 • taminarawley@xxx.com

OBJECTIVE

A position with a hardware/software engineering development group, utilizing my experience as an Engineering Assistant and Electronic Technician, where education is encouraged and supported.

SYSTEMS

• State-of-the-art micro-based stand-alone and multi-user workstations
• UNIX-based networked terminals

HARDWARE

• Computer engines
• Graphic terminals
• Graphic engines
• Memory controllers
• Mass storage units
• Displays

SOFTWARE

• UNIX
• Lotus SmartSuite
• MSDOS
• Microsoft Office

LANGUAGES

• AutoCAD
• Assembler
• C++
• Custom Micro-Code

EXPERIENCE
TEKTRONIX, Sacramento, CA, 1999-2003
Engineering Assistant/Support
Evaluated, qualified, and supported a wide range of workstation systems, graphic terminals, and mass storage systems by upgrading, performing failure analysis, repairing, and documenting information. Tested systems for environmental and mechanical specifications. Facilitated the ordering of equipment and parts to meet strict development timelines.

Senior Electronic Technician
Maintained and repaired workstation systems, graphic terminals, digital analysis systems, and storage displays. Implemented quality improvement projects that have trimmed process times in the manufacturing environment.

EDUCATION
1996-2000
Santa Clara University, Santa Clara, CA
Enrolled part-time in the Engineering Transfer Program
GPA 3.70/4.00

2004-present
B.S. degree March 2005
Albuquerque Technical Vocational Institute, Albuquerque, NM
Associate Degree in Electronic Technology
GPA 3.80/4.00

References provided on request

BARTHOLOMEW C. DECONCINI

723 S.W. Sixth Avenue
Detroit, MI 48112
(313) 555-9822
Bart.Deconcini@xxx.com

CAREER INTERESTS   A position with advancement potential in an engineering
                          environment that offers challenges and opportunity for
                          growth.

EDUCATION   Bachelor of Science Degree in Mechanical Engineering
                          Michigan State University, December 2003

DESIGN COURSEWORK   • Computer Aided Design (AutoCAD)
                          • Energy Efficient Building Design
                          • Heating, Ventilation, and Air-Conditioning--building
                            systems
                          • S.E.A program
                          • Power Plant Design--energy conversion systems
                          • Senior project--design, build, and race an entry in the
                            Society of Automotive Engineers Mini-Baja Competition

ANALYSIS COURSEWORK   • Applied Stress Analysis
                          • Materials Science
                          • Fluid Dynamics
                          • Vibration Analysis

COMPUTER EXPERIENCE   Numerical methods
                          Languages (Basic/FORTRAN)

PROFESSIONAL   Project Engineer, Midwest Irrigation Systems--Detroit, MI
WORK EXPERIENCE   January 2004 to present
                          Design and cost estimation of commercial and residential
                          irrigation systems.

REFERENCES   Letters of reference and a course grade summary are
                          available from:
                          Career Planning and Placement Center
                          Administrative Services Building
                          Michigan State University, East Lansing, MI 48824
                          (313) 555-1112

DERRICK W. JEFFERSON

27 WEST PANAMA, SAN DIEGO, CA 92132
(619) 555-4112
DERRICKJEFFERSON@XXX.COM

OBJECTIVE

A position as a Refinery Engineer for a major West Coast oil corporation.

PROFESSIONAL EXPERIENCE

CARIBBEAN OIL REFINING COMPANY, JAMAICA
REFINERY ENGINEER, 1998 TO 2004
Coordinator and inspector of various capital improvement and maintenance projects for offshore oil tanker jetties and refinery buildings.

MOBIL OIL COMPANY, SAN DIEGO, CA
CORPORATION ENGINEERING DEPARTMENT
PROJECT ENGINEER, 1993 TO 1998
Project engineer for developing feasibility studies, appropriation cost estimates, and designs for 15 to 20 diversified onshore and offshore projects.

MOBIL OIL COMPANY, SAN DIEGO, CA
OIL RECLAMATION DIVISION
REFINERY TECHNICIAN, 1989 TO 1993
Provided maintenance and troubleshooting for oil refineries in 17 states. Worked with engineers on design issues. Helped identify and repair major component malfunction on refinery equipment.

EDUCATION

B.S., Chemical Engineering, 1988
Pennsylvania State University, Hazleton, PA

PROFESSIONAL ASSOCIATIONS

• American Institute of Mining, Metallurgical, and Petroleum Engineering
• Association of Energy Engineers
• American Chemical Society

References and detailed project history available upon request.

JUNE ROETHE, P.E.

8276 N.E. 163rd Street • Portland, Oregon 97243 • (503) 555-1589
juneroethe@xxx.com

GOAL

To obtain an engineering position with a dynamic and growing company where I can use my analytical and computer skills to solve advanced engineering challenges.

EDUCATION

Master of Science, Mechanical Engineering
Portland State University, Portland, Oregon
• Currently working toward this degree; 75 percent completed; 4.0 GPA

Bachelor of Science, Mechanical Engineering
Portland State University, June 1999
• Achieved a 3.8 GPA in engineering coursework.
• Completed full year of computer science coursework beyond the engineering requirement.
• Completed extensive independent study in finite element analysis using the ANSYS analysis package.

Areas of academic interest:
• Machine design
• Finite element analysis
• Engineering application of microprocessors
• Automatic controls
• Computers in engineering

PROFESSIONAL EXPERIENCE

Project Engineer, ACME Robots and Manipulators, Portland, Oregon
November 2004 to present
• Responsible for new product development.
• Team leader for design of multitool hydraulic grinding manipulator for sale to Russia.
• Design hydraulic robot end effectors to meet customer specifications.
• Work with shop personnel to ensure ease of product manufacture and product costs within the budget.
• Selected CPU and 1/0 components and performed preliminary panel layout as part of design team for digital robot and manipulator controls.
• Implemented CAD system for engineering department.

PROFESSIONAL EXPERIENCE *(continued)*

Design Engineer, NDES Corporation, Mechanized Forest Products Division,
Tacoma, Washington
June 2003 to October 2004
- Designed hydraulically actuated attachments used for log skidding.
- Sole engineer responsible for designing new attachments that mount on crawler tractors.
- Created three-dimensional layout of design using a Computer Aided Design work station.
- Analyzed kinematics with classical and computer methods.
- Performed stress analysis with classical and finite element methods.
- Worked with manufacturing personnel to ensure low cost and ease of product manufacture.
- Verified attachment fit at dealerships where prototypes are mounted.
- Analyzed product performance by observing prototypes in the field.

COMPUTER EXPERTISE

Languages
- C
- Turbo Pascal
- Assembly
- FORTRAN
- Machine
- BASIC

Operating Systems
- MS-DOS
- VMS
- Windows
- MAC OSX

Software
- CADKEY (Computer Aided Design program)
- EXCEL spreadsheet
- AutoCAD
- Unigraphics
- NASTRAN (Finite Element Analysis package with GFEM for pre- and post-processing)
- Lotus Notes

PROFESSIONAL LICENSES

Professional Engineer, State of Oregon, 2005
EIT (Engineer-In-Training) exam passed, State of Washington, 2002

ACTIVITIES

President, Rose City Engineering Association, 2002-03
Chair, 1996 ASME Regional Conference
President, PSU ASME, 1995-96

REFERENCES

Will be provided upon request.

JOSEPH PETRI

103 Stoney Brook Drive
Milwaukee, WI 53023
(414) 555-0371
josephpetri@xxx.com

QUALIFICATIONS SUMMARY

More than seven years of civil engineering experience. More than nine years of project management experience coordinating the feasibility, design, and construction of diversified municipal and industrial projects. These projects have been accomplished on time and within budget.

PROFESSIONAL EXPERIENCE SUMMARY

Engineering Project Manager
2005 to present
Waste Management, Inc., Milwaukee, WI
Developed new business involving hazardous waste remedial services with targeted industries and operations throughout the Pacific Northwest.

Engineering Product Manager
1999 to 2005
Cabel Michel Corporation, Milwaukee, WI
Planned and implemented a sales/marketing program for Newfibre spunbonded, nonwoven geotextile fabrics for protection of impermeable synthetic membranes in ponds, reservoirs, and landfills. Generated more than $3 million in new business.

Project/Construction Manager
1994 to 1999
Harper-Wade Engineering, Inc., Chicago, IL
Served as Project/Construction Manager for the fast-track design and construction of a $24 million advanced wastewater treatment plant, resulting in a project time reduction of nine months and a project cost savings of more than $3 million. Also managed the permitting, design, and construction activities associated with development of a grass-roots oil refinery, a hydroelectric power plant, a saw chain manufacturing plant, and a semiconductor plant.

EDUCATION

Masters of Science, Civil Engineering, University of Wisconsin, 1994
Bachelor of Science, Civil Engineering, University of Wisconsin, 1992

PROFESSIONAL ASSOCIATIONS

• American Society of Civil Engineers
• Registered Professional Engineer

References Available Upon Request

DONALD S. SIMPSON

P.O. Box B235 • Louisville, KY 40231 • (502) 555-9219 • donaldsimpson@xxx.com

EXPERIENCE

General Manager
Waste Management, Inc., Louisville, KY
2002 to present
  Supervised all engineering and non-engineering staff members (48) at three solid waste treatment sites. Developed management plan for implementing coal-fired waste-to-energy facility. Served as chief engineer on design phase of project. Currently supervising construction phase.

President/Director
Environmental Resources Corporation, Memphis, TN, 2000 to 2002
  Responsible for the management of the business and its financing structure. Initially developed and implemented innovative technology for handling and processing municipal solid waste.

Engineering Manager/Vice President
Geometric Enterprises, Lexington, KY, 1996 to 1999
  Increasing responsibilities in the sales, design, and execution of various projects under contract with the EPA, primarily in the chemical plant and waste management areas. Also responsible for the evaluation of a number of waste treatment facilities.

Industrial Process Control Consultant
Midwest Chemical Industries, Ltd., Frankfort, KY, 1994 to 1996
  Undertook process control system design responsibility for a number of mineral processing plants being constructed by Midwest Chemical. This included the preparation of specifications, liaison with the clients, purchasing of equipment, and supervision of installation and start-up.

EDUCATION

Bachelor of Science Degree, University of Kentucky–2000
Waste Management Technology

Bachelor of Science Degree, University of Alberta, Edmonton–1996
Chemical Engineering, First Class Honors two years

ADDITIONAL DATA

Professional Engineer, states of Kentucky and Tennessee
Available to travel and relocate

References available upon request

• SHAWNA B. DAVIS •

Tel: (206) 555-1930
30266 Fraser Creek Drive
Vancouver, WA 98623
shawnadavis@xxx.com

• SUMMARY

Extensive experience with progressively greater responsibility in varied managerial, project engineering, and technical sales positions, with primary strengths in the areas of environmental technology, process equipment, industrial process control, engineering management, and written and verbal communications. Also, in-depth design and project experience in the waste management field including the design and operation of energy recovery and recycling processes, and in the chemical, mining, and iron and steel industries.

• OBJECTIVE

Project Manager/Project Engineer for industrial/municipal facility with focus on design, construction, and operation. Willing to relocate.

• EXPERIENCE

President/General Manager, 2003 to present
Waste Products Corporation, Vancouver, WA
Responsible for the commercial development and facility design for a newly developed technology that converts municipal solid waste into an inert lightweight aggregate. Also took on a variety of consulting projects.

Chief Instrumentation Engineer/Project Engineer, 2001 to 2003
Central Engineering Department, NACCO, Bellingham, WA
Responsible for coordinating the design, scheduling, procurement, and estimating activities for the preparation of feasibility studies for new mineral processing facilities in Australia and Indonesia. This included supervision of outside consultants and numerous field trips to gather site and other relevant data.

Sales Supervisor, Project Engineer, 1996 to 2001
Jenner & North, Inc., Seattle, WA
Responsible for the sale and execution of a number of major projects in the industrial automation field, primarily in the mining, iron ore pelletizing, steel, and power industries.

Page 1 of 2

- **EXPERIENCE** *(continued)*
Development Engineer, 1990 to 1996
Taysom Engineering, Boise, ID
Responsible for the coordination required between the owners, consultants, government planning agencies, contractors, and tenants on a number of commercial and industrial development projects.

- **EDUCATION**
Master of Science Degree, University of Washington, Seattle, 2000
Civil Engineering, Part-time Executive Program

Bachelor of Science Degree, University of Washington, Seattle, 1990
Electrical Engineering, Honors

- **ADDITIONAL INFORMATION**
  - Professional Engineer, Washington and Idaho
  - Computer literate in Windows and MS Office
  - Excellent oral and written communications
  - Proposal and business plan preparation

References available on request

REVA GOLDSTEIN

2215 S. Median Way, Reno, Nevada 89503
(702) 555-4498
revagoldstein@xxx.com

PROFESSIONAL OBJECTIVE

Seeking a management position emphasizing acquired skills, education, and experience in the energy industry, including:
• General Management
• Operations Management
• Technical Management

QUALIFICATIONS AND ACHIEVEMENTS

More than 15 years of engineering management experience with primary emphasis and expertise in the following areas:

ENGINEERING OPERATIONS MANAGEMENT
• Large, complex project direction, coordination, and definition
• Strategic long/short-range planning
• Site selection and facilities/plant set-up
• Specific expertise in drilling, mining operations

PERSONNEL MANAGMENET
• Personnel recruitment and performance evaluation
• Salary negotiation and administration
• Fostering creative, cooperative, and productive employees
• Relationships in a disciplined work environment

PROFESSIONAL EXPERIENCE

NEVADA DEPARTMENT OF ENVIRONMENTAL QUALITY, Reno, Nevada
Engineering Specialist (January 2003 to Present)
Conduct Superfund hazardous waste site preliminary assessments and site investigations. Monitor remediation activities and response actions; review technical, design, and other engineering documents. Regulator for state and federal hazardous and solid waste laws and regulations.

Page 1 of 2

PROFESSIONAL EXPERIENCE *(continued)*

DENVER OIL PRODUCTION COMPANY, Denver, Colorado, 1996 to 2003
Technical Advisor to the Regional Staff (1998 to 2003)
Monitored major drilling projects and coordinated corporate technical information. Involved with troubleshooting and quota evaluations.

Geologist, Group Supervisor (1996 to 1998)
Supervised 28 professionals and support staff. Formulated budgets, salary administration, project definition, and exploration strategy.

EDUCATION

UNIVERSITY OF NEVADA, Las Vegas, Nevada
Bachelor of Science in Engineering Technology, 1995
Minors: Geology/Industrial Management

COLORADO SCHOOL OF MINES, Golden, Colorado
Department of Environmental Engineering
Completed intensive 29-week program, 2002

•References Available Upon Request

MOISHA V. DAHRENS
ENGINEERING CONSULTANT

225 Austin Avenue SW, Suite 13
Houston, TX 77012
(713) 555-0277
moishadahrens@xxx.com

OBJECTIVE
Seeking employment with growth-oriented engineering consulting firm, specializing in energy, chemical, and transportation industries.

SUMMARY OF PROJECT EXPERIENCE
- Developed procedures, checklists, and training protocols for implementing preloading inspections of rail tank cars and tank motor vehicles at DuPont manufacturing facilities.
- Led a geodetic engineering team to evaluate available toxic gas release computer models; acquired and improved a state-of-the-art modeling capability for DuPont and directed its application to DuPont facilities.
- Participated in environmental and safety compliance audits for numerous DuPont refineries, manufacturing facilities, wholesale terminals, and upstream production facilities in the United States.
- Coordinated SEC environmental liabilities reporting for the Standard Oil Company, prior to the DuPont buy-out.
- Coordinated the establishment and propagation of the Chemical Education for Public Understanding Program (CEPUP) in school systems in Texas via DuPont grant funding to the University of Texas at Austin.
- Coordinated DuPont's annual Engineering Expenditures Forecast, working with engineering departments in 27 manufacturing sites throughout the United States.

EMPLOYMENT HISTORY
Senior Engineering Specialist, DuPont Southwest Region, Houston, TX
January 2001 to present

Engineering Specialist, Standard Oil Company, Energy Division, Austin, TX
September 1996 to December 2000

EDUCATION
Bachelor of Science Degree, Chemical Engineering, University of Texas, San Antonio, 1996

Certification, Geodetic Engineering, Professional Training Program, University of Texas, Houston, 2004

References available on request

Cal Fremont

127 Centerfield Drive, #23 • San Diego, California 92126
(619) 555-2497 • calfremont@xxx.com

Professional Summary

More than 12 years of domestic and international experience in project management, engineering design, and construction supervision related to hydroelectric power, mining, and heavy civil projects.

Professional Experience

Marshfield Development Corp., San Diego, California
Project Director, March 2001 to present

> Managed multidisciplinary engineering effort and supervised constructability reviews during preparation of design criteria, methodology, construction plans, and specifications for the Pacific Northwest National Gas Transmission System. Developed field surveillance and construction monitoring plans, reviewed Quality Control and Quality Assurance plans, and directly supervised construction of Northern Border and Pacific Transmission lines within system. Managed budget, subcontractors, schedules, and cost.

Senior Project Engineer, September 1996 to March 2001

> Management and construction supervision of the Mission Hill hydroelectric project, which included concrete and earth dams, control weirs and diversion tunnel, railway cuts, embankments, and bridges. Responsibility involved contract management, application of specifications, documents for tender, liaison with clients and public. Supervised rock and earth excavation, construction of coffer dams and grout curtain, installation of piezometer, pressure relief system, rock bolts, slope indicators, and other instrumentation.

> Supervised compaction and testing for earth dikes, concrete pouring and testing, and installation of dewatering systems. Also responsible for schedule, cost, and change orders. Assisted in design and construction supervision of many other projects, including:
> • Rail and road tunnel beneath a navigational canal
> • Four-lane highway tunnel, stretching two miles in granite
> • Shipyard in southern Chile
> • Highway bridges in Puerto Rico
> • Hydroelectric power projects in Kenya, Argentina, and the West Indies

Education

B.S., Civil Engineering, University of California at San Diego, 1995
Post-graduate certification training, Civil Engineering, UCSD, 1996

References

Available, with detailed project descriptions, upon request.

Dana M. Keizer

2640 Maitland Circle SE
Hackensack, NJ 07603
(201) 555-3421
danakeizer@xxx.com

Objective

An advancement opportunity within a major engineering firm, with responsibility for project management and direction.

Skills and Experience

- Extensive background in engineering management and design of oil and gas pipelines, water resources, and hazardous waste management.
- Served as co-director for several major civil projects, including water, gas, and oil pipeline system design and construction.
- Experienced with managing business operations, profit centers, management information systems, and acquisitions.
- Managed responsibility for developing design standards and supervising implementation of quality control systems.
- Directly involved with site investigations and remediation designs for various project sites.
- Assisted with site characterization, feasibility studies, and risk assessments.

Employment Summary

Northeast Development Corp.--Newark, NJ--2003 to Present
Director of Technical Services, Engineering Division

DaVor Industries, Inc.--Allentown, PA--1997 to 2003
Engineer, Special Projects Section

DaVor Industries, Inc.--Wilmington, DE--1996 to 1997
Civil Engineering Intern

Education

University of Pittsburgh--Pittsburgh, PA
B.S. Degree, Civil Engineering, 1997

Memberships

- Registered Professional Engineer in New Jersey, Pennsylvania, and Delaware
- Member, Geotechnical Society of America
- Association of Civil and Mechanical Engineers

References on request.

TALBOT HUNTER

Rte. 6E, Stop 1156 • Chugiak, Alaska 99623 • (907) 555-3911 • talbothunter@xxx.com

PROFESSIONAL OBJECTIVE

An engineering management position with a firm specializing in civil projects.

PROFESSIONAL EXPERIENCE

Director of Technical Services
Al-Can Engineering, Ltd., Anchorage, Alaska, 2003 to present
Supervised technical operations for regional offices in Alaska, British Columbia, and Alberta. Responsible for developing design standards, implementing project management and project control systems, and supervising construction at project sites. Worked with senior technical experts from all divisions, including chief engineer, chief hydrogeologist, chief compliance officer, chief construction manager, and the directors of bioremediation technology and health and safety.

Executive Engineer
Mentor GeoSystems, Inc., Anchorage, Alaska, 2000 to 2003
Prepared environmental impact statement, terrain sensitivity report, and design of river-crossing constructs. Prepared design manual for drainage and erosion control for Yukon Lateral Pipeline. Prepared final geotechnical report for submission to the federal government on the design and construction of the Trans-Canada natural gas pipeline.

Engineering Specialist
CH2M Hill, Engineering Consultants, Denver, Colorado, 1996 to 2000
Reviewed geologic, hydrologic, geotechnical, and thermal design for Trans-Canada natural gas pipeline. Assisted in establishing criteria for environmental protection, erosion control procedures, foundations, slope stability, surface and groundwater hydrology, design of drainage structures, and general civil construction techniques. Conducted detailed review of quality control plans. Provided on-site monitoring and technical assistance. Began employment as intern and was hired full-time upon degree completion.

EDUCATION

B.S., Civil Engineering, cum laude, University of Colorado, Denver, 1996
Founding member of student chapter of the American Society of Civil Engineers; served two years as president. Initiated program for on-site training and student internships with several local engineering firms, in cooperation with the College of Engineering.

References Available Upon Request.

TINA CHOVANEK

1735 N. Paloma Boulevard

Charleston, SC 29401

Cell: (803) 555-2481

Email: tinachovanek@xxx.com

OBJECTIVE

Mechanical engineering position that draws upon my knowledge of engineering and my technical skills.

SUMMARY

- Ambitious, self-starting mechanical engineer with two and a half years' experience in mechanical design.
- Excellent reputation for integrating manufacturing requirements into design.
- Highly motivated and dependable person who is an excellent source for new ideas.
- Sincere commitment in learning new skills and accepting new responsibilities.

EDUCATION

Bachelor of Mechanical Engineering Technology, Purdue University, May 1999

PROFESSIONAL EXPERIENCE

CapCom Coin-Op, Inc., Charleston, SC, July 2004 to Present
Mechanical Engineer
- Design small mechanisms, vacuum form and injection molded plastics, sheet metal and wire form parts for pinball games.
- Work from concepts through full production.
- Interact with suppliers and vendors on first article inspection of parts.
- Directly responsible for solid design completion with complete documentation package, plus B.O.M. for all design assignments.
- Oversaw mechanism life testing.
- Modified and added Autolisp programs as needed.
- Updated and maintained drawings per ECNs.

PROFESSIONAL EXPERIENCE *(CONTINUED)*

Paltier, Inc., Charleston, SC, March 2004 to July 2004
Mechanical Engineer (contract position)
- Designed industrial rack systems and modular mezzanine systems for industrial manufacturers.
- Analyzed load distribution and systems strength for vast situations.
- Developed product quotations for sales and distributors.
- Worked hand-in-hand with sales to ensure they had proper knowledge of our products.
- Created detailed documentation packages of industrial rack and mezzanine systems.
- Updated and maintained drawings per ECNs.

COMPUTER EXPERIENCE

Hardware: IBM PCs and clones
Software: AutoCAD with 3-D knowledge and Windows applications

References available on request.

Thomas J. Zamir

7715 Weston Park Lane • Charlotte, NC 28214
(704) 555-2866 • ThomasZamir@xxx.com

Education

B.S., Industrial Management, Milwaukee School of Engineering, May 1996
A.A.S., Industrial Engineering Technology, Milwaukee School of Engineering, May 1994
Pre-Engineering Studies, Rock Valley College, 1990–1992
Machine Trades 1-4, Rockford Area Vocational Center, 1988–1990

Experience

Snap-On Tools--Bensenville, IL
4/03–Present
Research and development facility developing new processes and materials for Snap-On Tools.

Senior Process Engineer
- Design and try out new fixtures
- Develop tooling for new equipment being purchased
- Research new manufacturing methods for implementation
- Computer support for PCs and network

Forgings & Stampings, Inc.--Rockford, IL
3/00–4/03
Small hydraulic-hammer shop with hammers ranging in size from 1,000 lbs. to 4,000 lbs., producing carbon steel forgings in many shapes.

Engineering/Quality Manager
- Set up CAD system for tooling design
- Set up a print control system
- Started a gauge calibration program
- Implemented S.P.C. checking
- Troubleshooting of processes
- Equipment troubleshooting

Rockford Drop Forge--Rockford, IL
4/99–3/00
Medium-size steam-powered-hammer shop with hammers ranging in size from 1,500 lbs. to 4,000 lbs., producing mostly carbon steel and stainless forgings.

Tool Design Engineer
- Designed forge tooling to customer's specifications
- Floor troubleshooting of new and existing tooling
- Worked with tool room and outside contractors making tools
- Upgraded both hardware and software on CAD system

Experience (continued)

Teledyne Portland Forge--Lebanon, KY
9/98–4/99
New start-up facility utilizing three screw presses in a cellular set-up press. Sizes ranged from 1,600 to 2,500 tons and produced both carbon and alloy steel forgings. Initial start-up date 6/97.
Product Design Engineer
- Designed forge and trim tooling for quick die change holders
- Worked with continuous improvement teams
- Troubleshooting of process problems on the floor

Teledyne Portland Forge--Portland, IN
5/97–8/98
Large forging facility utilizing both power hammers and upset equipment ranging in size from 1,000 lbs. to 2,500 lbs. on the hammers and from 6≤ down to 2≤ on the upsetters.
Product Design Engineer
- Designed forge tooling for the hammers and all secondary operations required to make the parts
- Troubleshooting of floor problems associated with tooling; worked with tool room and department managers in designing and changing tooling
- Our department responsible for designing approximately 200 new tools a year not including changes and revisions

Anchor-Harvey Components, Inc.--Freeport, IL
3/93–5/97
Medium-size press forging operation utilizing both mechanical and screw presses ranging in size from 250 to 1,200 tons, producing aluminum and brass forgings in many sizes and shapes.
Manufacturing Engineer
- Developed and implemented a routing and bill of material for each part produced
- Member of MRP project team responsible for implementing MRP into the plant
- Responsible for ordering and scheduling new and repaired tooling
- Worked with customers to design forgings to fit their applications
- Justified the purchase of and set up CAD system

Computer Skills

- Basic and COBOL programming languages
- Catia, CadKey, AutoCAD, and AutoTrol system 7000 CAD software
- Many other PC/DOS/Windows-based software programs
- PC repair and building as a hobby

References on request

Sandra G. Patterson

77 W. 13th Street • Salt Lake City, UT 84121
(801) 555-2241 • spatterson@xxx.com

Career Objective

Entry-level engineering technology position in the field of industrial processes with an opportunity to train toward project management.

Education

Associate of Science Degree, Engineering Technology, 1998
New Mexico State University, Las Cruces, NM

Currently working toward Bachelor of Science Degree in Industrial Engineering at the University of Utah, Salt Lake City, UT; 70 percent completed.

Fields of Study:

- Industrial Processes
- Circuit Theory
- Concrete and Soil Technology
- Electronic Circuits
- Production and Quality Control
- Systems Analysis
- Fluid Technology

- Control Systems
- Applied Mechanics
- Applied Design
- Thermal Power
- Applied Strength of Materials
- Plant Design
- Industrial Applications

Special Projects

- Participated in team research program at local industrial processing plant.
- Served as team leader for plant analysis phase of project.
- Worked closely with industrial engineers and specialists in systems engineering.
- Assisted faculty member in development of lab technology program in electronic circuits lab.
- Prepared final paper that was submitted to state office of accreditation for approval.

Employment

Sales Associate, Radio Shack, Salt Lake City, UT
2000 to present
- Handle questions regarding product information and operation.
- Make sales of electronic equipment including computers, telephones, facsimile machines, and cables and components for do-it-yourself electronics projects.

References available upon request.

GINA A. PASTEGA

2125 N.W. Peoria Road • Burlington, Iowa 52602
(319) 555-3976 • ginapastega@xxx.com

OBJECTIVE

Seeking employment in the field of chemical engineering where I can put my education to practical use for the benefit of a Midwest chemical corporation.

EDUCATION

Bachelor of Science Degree, expected December 2005
Chemical Engineering with minor in Pharmaceutical Science
Ball State University, Muncie, Indiana
Cumulative GPA 3.56; Major/Minor GPA 3.87

KNOWLEDGE AND SKILLS

Chemical Engineering Analysis

Experienced in laboratory and computer-aided analysis of chemical models for heat transfer, mass transfer, fluid flow, corrosion, and corrosion control. Also prepared critical evaluation of models and solutions for problems in process flow sheeting, transport phenomena, reaction engineering, separations, and process dynamics.

Chemical Plant Design and Chemical Reaction Engineering

Developed small-scale model of design for chemical plant; worked on design of chemical engineering equipment and developed working prototypes. Studied the design of chemical reactors, making comparisons of performance and economic evaluations of reactor types, with emphasis on single-phase reacting systems.

Process Design and Control

Examined modern control theory and applied it to chemical systems. Determined optimal design and operation of chemical processing systems, including large-scale and large number of variable type problems, mathematical methods, process modeling, constrained optimization, and planning and scheduling problems.

Pharmaceutical Science

Experienced in applying quantitative methods, both chemical and physical, to pharmaceuticals and their dosage forms. Gained understanding of influence of pharmaceutical formulations on bio-availability of drugs, as well as principles of pharmacology, toxicity, and pharmacokinetics.

WORK HISTORY

Student Intern, January to March 2005
Rexall Drug Store Pharmacy, Burlington, Iowa
On-the-job training in application of pharmaceuticals.

References available on request.

Paul E. Everett

Current Address:
7A West Hall, Providence College
Providence, RI 02028
(401) 555-1242

Permanent Address:
8224 S. Marine Parade
Baltimore, MD 21217
(301) 555-0112

Objective

Seeking a position in agricultural engineering with an organization working in irrigation and resources machinery.

Educational Background

Bachelor of Science Degree, June 2005
Providence College, Providence, RI
Major: Agricultural Engineering; Minor: Irrigation Engineering

Courses of Study

Irrigation System Design:
- Soil physics and plant water use applied to irrigation system design.
- Design of gravity, pressurized, and trickle systems; improving on-farm water management; performance characteristics of pumps and other irrigation equipment.

Soil and Water Conservation Engineering:
- Design of on-farm water supply and distribution systems, including wells, pipelines, and open channel flow.
- Hydraulics of soil profiles; design of drainage systems.
- Salinity management in agricultural production systems.

Biological Systems Modeling:
- Development of functional relationships using interpolation, regression, and cubic splines; development of models; stimulation of random processes; optimization techniques.

Design in Agricultural Engineering:
- The practice of engineering design; logical steps in the design process; emphasis on team approach to design and problem definition.

Courses of Study *(continued)*

Agricultural Structures and Environment:
- Load distribution, construction, and duration analysis; wood and reinforced concrete design; heat and moisture balancers; fasteners; mechanical and natural ventilation design; regular and controlled atmospheric storage.

Computers in Problem Solving:
- Engineering, physics, and chemistry problems solved through the use of sophisticated engineering software.

Other courses included:
- Design of Biological Resources Machinery, Groundwater Modeling, Applied Hydrology, Sediment Transport, Water Resources Analysis.

Employment History

Lab Assistant, Hydrology Laboratory
September 2002 to present
Providence College, Providence, RI

References

Available on request

■ D'YLYNN KONDO

P.O. Box 1983
Williston, North Dakota 58801
(701) 555-2496
D-Kondo@xxx.com

CAREER OBJECTIVE

To obtain an entry-level position as an engineering scientist with a large Midwest corporation.

EDUCATIONAL EXPERIENCE

B.S. in Engineering Science
Ottawa University, Ottawa, Kansas
December 2004 (GPA 3.75)

ELECTRICAL FUNDAMENTALS

- Electric theory laws.
- Circuit analysis of DC circuits.
- Natural, step, and sinusoidal responses of circuits.
- Operational amplifier characteristics and applications.
- Laboratory experimentation and analysis.

STATICS

- Analysis of forces induced in structures and machines by various types of loading.
- Involved in experimental processes under supervision of and in cooperation with graduate researcher.

DYNAMICS

- Kinematics, Newton's laws of motion, and work-energy and impulse-momentum relationships applied to engineering systems.

STRENGTH OF MATERIALS

- Properties of structural materials.
- Analysis of stress and deformation in axially loaded members, circular shafts, and beams, and in statically indeterminate systems containing these components.

EDUCATIONAL EXPERIENCE (continued)
THERMODYNAMICS
■ Closed and open control systems.
■ Thermodynamic theory, laws, properties; thermodynamic cycles, phase and chemical equilibria, and gas dynamics.

MATERIALS SCIENCE
■ Structure and properties of metals, ceramics, and organic materials.
■ Control of structure during processing and structural modification by service environment.
■ Mechanical behavior of materials, relating laboratory results to material structure and elements of mechanical analysis.

MOMENTUM, ENERGY, AND MASS TRANSFER
■ Control volume and differential analysis of fluid flow; momentum transfer; conductive, convective, and radiative energy transfer; binary mass transfer; and prediction of transport qualities.

References and official transcripts available on request.

JANE S. MILES

P.O. Box 128 • Linden, AL 36748
205-555-2095
Jane_Miles@xxx.com

Objective

To obtain an entry-level position in chemical engineering within the paper or synthetic fibers industry.

Education

Bachelor of Science Degree, Chemical Engineering, 2004
Purdue University, West Lafayette, IN

Areas of Experience

Convective Heat Transfer: Effects of convective heat transfer in gas solid systems; application to design of heat transfer equipment.

Experimental Laboratory Experience

Chemical Reactors: Design, performance, and scale of reactors involving solids (packed, fluidized, trickle, and slurry reactors) and without solids (gas/liquid absorbers, biochemical systems, non-ideal flow, polymerization systems).

Chemical Engineering Thermodynamics: Application of fundamental laws of thermodynamics to complex systems. Properties of solutions of non-electrolytes.

Phase and Chemical Equilibrium: Chemical reaction equilibrium analysis and modeling for aqueous electrolyte solutions. Methods of estimating properties. Availability analysis.

Process Control: Analog and digital control methods and control strategies in the chemical process industries.

Special Projects

- Design and development of prototype heater/cooler method for stabilizing materials in production of high-opacity paper.
- Co-authored report to be printed in *Chemical Engineering Abstracts* in July 2005.
- Honors project on the application of convective heat transfer properties to design of equipment to measure levels of condensation in paper production processes.

Work Experience

Print Shop Technician, 2000 to 2002
Magnolia Printing & Copy Center, Mobile, AL
- Worked as press operator on four-color sheet-fed printing press.
- Assisted with paper selection and purchasing.
- Familiar with basic properties of commercial-grade papers for printing.

References and transcripts will be provided upon request.

David Allison

227 Winston Avenue
New Bedford, MA 02711
(413) 555-2719
davidallison@xxx.com

Summary

- Quick learner and a smart worker, able to bring my skills to immediate use in any environment.
- Very successful in dealing with a multitude of different personalities, and my strongest skill is working with people.
- Excellent references, which will be supplied upon request.
- Although most of my experience thus far has been in the manufacturing industry, am looking forward to using my degree in business administration to expand my scope of work.

Education

Bachelor of Science, Business Administration, Indiana Wesleyan University, 2003
Associate of Science, Industrial Engineering Technology, Purdue University, 1999

Experience

Maintenance Supervisor, Visteon Ford, East Faith Haven, MA, 2003–Present
- Supervise 15-20 skilled tradesmen while ensuring that multimillion-dollar equipment is repaired in a timely fashion.
- Maintain orderly records on repair and replacement of equipment.
- Order parts for equipment.
- Maintain pay records for employees.
- Work without direct supervision on an off-shift seven days a week.
- Work directly with production via two-way radio.
- Clean and stock maintenance work areas.
- Attend cost-reduction meetings.
- Directly responsible for keeping more than 85 pieces of machinery running.
- Multitask prioritization.

Experience
(continued)

Industrial Engineer, SteelWorks, Inc., Oxford, MA, 2000–2003
• Submitted and implemented cost reduction ideas.
• Purchased new machinery, performed cost estimation, quoted new business to potential customers, and conducted many time and motion studies.
• Assisted in plant layout with project engineering.
• Assisted in design of product with design engineering.
• Created and maintained routings and bill of material files on AS/400 system.
• Assisted in MRP with production scheduler.
• Worked with purchasing manager on ordering raw materials.
• Developed new packing and shipping standards.
• Supervised department secretary.
• Trained many assistants on use of AS/400 and department procedures.

Service Engineer, Vacuum Instrument Corporation, Harborview, MA, 1997–2000
• Installed and repaired leak detection equipment.
• Traveled to many different companies in different states and assessed problems with and repaired or replaced equipment.
• Filled out expense reports and maintained budgets.
• Dealt with irate customers in their environment.

Industrial Engineer, Dresser Industries, Weir Village, MA, Summer 1997
• Performed time study, assisted with plant layout, created and maintained database files, and kept detailed records on operation of equipment.

References on request.

Parker Jameson

116 S.E Decker Terrace • Omaha, Nebraska 68101
(402) 555-0221 • parkerjameson@xxx.com

Professional Goal

To obtain entry-level employment in civil engineering with an organization involved in environmental management or conservation issues.

Educational Experience and Training

B.S. in Civil Engineering with Minor in Environmental Engineering, June 2005
University of Omaha, Nebraska

Engineering Qualifications

Completed college-level training in the following subject areas:
• Civil and Construction Engineering
• Fluid Mechanics
• Hydraulic Engineering
• Civil Engineering Materials
• Engineering Planning
• Modern Construction Methods
• Civil Engineering Design
• Applied Structural Analysis
• Probabilistic Structural Engineering

Environmental Qualifications

Completed college-level training in the following subject areas:
• Environmental Engineering Fundamentals
• Applied Hydrology, Water Resources Design, Ocean Engineering
• Technology and Environmental Systems
• Ports and Harbors
• Air Pollution Control
• Environmental Assessment
• Earth Structures
• Fate, Transport, and Control of Hazardous Substances
• Designing with Geotextiles
• Soil Improvement, Soil Dynamics, Engineering Property of Soils
• Applied Soil Mechanics
• Water Quality Dynamics
• Chemistry of Environmental Systems
• Microbial Processes in Environmental Systems

References and course descriptions/transcripts available upon request.

DARRYL A. MacKENZIE
442 N.W. Sunset Place
Corvallis, Oregon 97330
(503) 555-9227
Darrylmackenzie@xxx.com

CAREER OBJECTIVE
Civil engineering staff position in corporation or government organization responsible for large-scale civil construction projects.

DEGREE ACHIEVED
B.S. Degree in Civil Engineering, 2004
Oregon State University, Corvallis, Oregon
Graduated 15th in class of 221; GPA 3.92

SPECIALTY COURSES COMPLETED
- Highway Engineering
- Highway Location and Design
- Reinforced Concrete Construction
- Low-Volume Road Design
- Asphalt Technology
- Advanced Concrete Technology
- Traffic Flow Analysis and Control
- Public Transportation Facility Design
- Transportation Systems Analysis and Planning
- Pre-stressed Concrete
- Traffic Operations and Design
- Bridge Design
- Construction Engineering Management and Methods
- Pavement Evaluation and Management
- Municipal Planning and Urban Engineering

EXPERIENCE
Student Internship, Summer 2002
State of Oregon Highway Division
- Worked with highway engineers on traffic pattern study and analysis.
- Conducted research in current traffic management theory and technology.
- Prepared written report for presentation to chief highway engineer.
- Assisted with planning and preparation for public hearings on proposed change in traffic flow.

References on request.

STEPHEN FAIRFIELD

P.O. Box 55
Santa Barbara, CA 93102
(805) 555-0993
stephenfairfield@xxx.com

Professional Objective

Seeking a position as engineering specialist with the engineering division of a major petroleum corporation.

Educational Training

Bachelor of Science Degree, March 2005
Civil Engineering with extensive coursework in Ocean Engineering
University of California at Santa Barbara

Courses Completed
- Fluid Mechanics I, II
- Hydraulic Engineering I, II, III
- Hydrology I, II, III
- Ocean Engineering I, II, III
- Water Resources Design I, II
- Structural Theory and Advanced Structural Theory
- Ports and Harbors: Design and Construction Methods
- Photo Interpretation (with special study in interpretation of LANDSAT imagery)
- Photogrammetry
- Applied Structural Analysis
- Water Quality Dynamics
- Contemporary Engineering Technology
- Dynamics of Ocean Structures
- Applied Ocean and Coastal Engineering
- Ocean Engineering Wave Mechanics
- Random Wave Mechanics
- Ocean Instrumentation and Control Theory
- Wave Forces on Structures
- Coastal and Estuarine Hydrodynamics
- Ocean and Coastal Engineering Measurements
- Finite Amplitude Wave Mechanics
- Marine Geotechnical Engineering Special Study

Prepared report on safety issues and design and construction solutions for off-shore oil drilling platforms. Published in *Ocean Engineering Journal*, vol. 15, no. 3, January 2002, pp. 137–139.

References and complete course descriptions and grade transcripts will be provided on request.

HALIMEDA SHILAOS

2212 Seminole Street • Tampa, FL 33612
813-555-4356 (days) • 813-555-2592 (evenings)
halimedashilaos@xxx.com

CAREER OBJECTIVE

Project management position with large-scale construction projects for major engineering firm.

EDUCATIONAL BACKGROUND

Bachelor of Science Degree, awarded June 2004
Construction Engineering Management/Civil Engineering
University of South Florida

Specific Areas of Training Completed

- Civil Engineering: Core requirements in civil and construction engineering, mechanics, statistics, strength of materials, civil engineering design fundamentals, engineering economics, physics, calculus, materials science.
- Construction Engineering Management: Plane surveying, fundamentals of estimating, dynamics for construction, fluid mechanics and hydraulics, construction estimating, construction project management, civil engineering materials, soils in engineering, structural theory, structural problems management, highway and road location and design, construction management, electrical and mechanical facilities, contracts and specifications.
- Management and Business Principles: Management science, fundamentals of accounting, quantitative business methods, business law, legal issues in construction seminar, economics, business finance, managing organizations, accounting for decision making, management and labor.

EXPERIENCE

Student Intern, Summer/Fall 2002
Barry Brothers Engineering and Construction, Inc., Tampa, FL

- Worked full-time under the supervision of the chief engineer on a major office complex construction project.
- Assisted in all areas of project management, including budgeting, scheduling, personnel management, record keeping, communications, and on-site management.

Framer, Summers 2000–2001
Castleton Construction, Tampa, FL

- Worked full-time as a framer for a residential construction company. Participated in the construction of more than 36 homes, including a 5,500-square-foot, three-story structure and an 1,800-square-foot dome.

References available on request.

PETRA A. GALASHEN

98-A Huntington Park Drive
Long Beach, California 90822
Cell: (213) 555-4493
Email: Petra.Galashen@xxx.com

CAREER GOAL

Entry-level position in the research and development department of an electronics manufacturing firm. Opportunities for advancement an essential element.

EDUCATION

B.S. in Electrical and Electronics Engineering
University of California, Los Angeles, 2004

AREAS OF CONCENTRATION

Electronic Materials and Devices:

Fundamentals of semiconductors, mathematical models, PN junction operation, and device characteristics.

Electromechanical Energy Conversion:

Non-linear magnetic circuits. Saturable reactors and transformers. Voltage generation and energy conversion for electromechanical devices. Characteristics of electromechanical machines.

Semiconductors:

Semiconductor devices. Theories of PN and Schottky junctions. MOSFET, MESFET, JFET, and bipolar transistors. Theory and practice of semiconductor processing techniques. Semiconductor physics relevant for advanced use of semiconductor materials and devices. Quantum mechanics and solid-state physics. Two- and three-terminal semiconductor electronic devices.

AREAS OF CONCENTRATION (continued)

Digital Electronics:

Switching in electronic devices and circuits. Design and analysis of circuits in digital systems. Interconnections and noise problems. Theory and design of digital integrated circuits, including CMOS and bipolar logic. Analysis and design of digital integrated circuits. Digital signal processing. Optimum filter design, declamation and interpolation methods, quantization error effects, and spectral estimation.

WORK EXPERIENCE

Lab Technician, Electronics Laboratory, UCLA College of Engineering
September 2002 to June 2004

- Worked with lab manager to maintain equipment and supplies, supervise lab sessions for pre-engineering students, and conduct equipment testing and servicing.

Library Aide, UCLA Engineering Library
October 2000 to September 2002

- Worked in circulation department.
- Responded to queries from library patrons.
- Shelved books and periodicals.
- Worked 25 hours per week in addition to full course load.
- Worked full-time during summers.

References provided upon request.

carole van sant

336 Pritchard Street SE • Wichita, Kansas 67204
316-555-0118 • carolevansant@xxx.com

professional objective
Entry-level position with growth-oriented computer design and manufacturing corporation.

educational experience
Bachelor of Science Degree in Computer Engineering, 2004
University of Arizona, Tucson, Arizona

course topics
- Calculus, Vector Calculus, and Differential Equations
- Statistics and Dynamics Data Structures, FORTRAN, COBOL, UNIX, and C
- Electric and Magnetic Fields
- Electronic Materials and Devices
- Electronic Circuits and Digital Electronics
- Signals and Systems
- Computer Organization and System Design

microprocessor applications
- Computer architecture
- VLSI design techniques
- Computer operating systems and data acquisition
- Semiconductor processes, design, devices
- Power electronics
- Designed and built personal computers, utilizing available materials in electronics laboratory with only a minor cost investment
- Wrote program that tests speed of microprocessor circuitry in nanoseconds
- Prepared written report and sample operations for completion of senior honors project

work history
Central Computer Stores, Inc., Tucson, Arizona
Sales Associate, 2002 to present
- Serve clientele in high-volume computer sales outlet store
- Demonstrate equipment and software products

References and transcripts available on request

✦ RUBY J. SANDERS ✦

P.O. BOX 58, WELLS, NV 89835 • (702) 555-3357 • rubysanders@xxx.com

✦ OBJECTIVE

An internship with an organization involved with resource management or conservation.

✦ EDUCATION

Currently working toward Bachelor of Science degree in Minerals Engineering at the Colorado School of Mines, Golden, CO. Anticipated completion date, June 2006.

Courses Include:
- Mining Technology
- Metallurgical Engineering
- Mining Engineering
- Hydrology
- Instrumentation
- Computational Fluid Dynamics
- Environmental Engineering
- Mining Waste Treatment
- Chemical Structures Engineering

✦ EXPERIENCE

Assistant Night Manager
Dale's In and Out Drive-In, Wells, NV
September 2003 to present
   Responsibilities Include:
- Customer service and sales
- Accurate cash tallies and inventory reports
- Sole management of swing shift for small 24-hour restaurant
- Personnel management and scheduling
- Knowledge of all aspects of small restaurant operation

Minerals Management Volunteer
Rocky Mountain National Forest, Central District, Mountain City, CO
July to September 2003
   Responsibilities Included:
- Assisting forester in inspecting mining activities
- Monitoring reclamation and aspen regeneration studies
- Helping with recreation projects and administration
- Performing minor maintenance duties
- Participating in groundwater studies

References available on request.

GEOFFREY W. LAWRENCE
443 S. 26th Street, Apt. 21 • Salina, KS 67401
913-555-8861 • geoffreylawrence@xxx.com

CAREER GOAL

Entry-level position in computer engineering at a major electronics manufacturer.

EDUCATION

B.S. in Computer Engineering, Kansas Wesleyan University, December 2004
Engineering program at KWU is E.A.C./A.B.E.T. accredited
Degree conferred with highest honors

AREAS OF ACADEMIC SPECIALIZATION

Dynamic System Simulation

- Digital, analog, and hybrid computer simulation of dynamic systems described by ordinary differential and difference equations.

Computer Architecture

- Design techniques for the synthesis of digital computers.
- Principles of computer structure and design as applied to major computer functions.
- Internal organization and application of microprocessors and microcomputers.
- Design process for microprocessor systems, VLSI design theory and practice.
- Design, layout, and simulation of a complete VLSI chip using CAD tools.

Electronic Materials

- Physics and chemistry of electronic materials and methods of materials characterization.
- Technology, theory, and analysis of processing methods used in integrated circuit fabrication.
- Advanced treatment of two- and three-terminal semiconductor electronic devices, microwave, and optical devices.

Integrated Circuits

- Analysis and design of analog and digital integrated circuits. Advanced methods in digital, stochastic, and analog signal processing systems and system designs.

MEMBERSHIPS

Student Chapter, Institute of Electrical and Electronics Engineers
Student Chapter, National Action Council for Minorities in Engineering

REFERENCES PROVIDED ON REQUEST

Jerrold H. Carter

3220 Harrison Road
Austin, Texas 78759
512-555-2436
jerroldcarter@xxx.com

EDUCATION

Greenville College
B.A. cum laude, Mathematics, 1998
Greenville, Illinois

Technical:

The Cambridge Institute for Computer Programming
Certificate, 2000
Boston, Massachusetts

PROFESSIONAL EXPERIENCE

IBM, Austin, Texas
Consultant Contractor/System Developer, 10/03–Present
Contract developer on-site at IBM. Architect of system implementation of a Smalltalk/VPM application of an OS/2 PM-based computer network configuration system developed and marketed by IBM. Worked on project team of twenty as lead implementation designer and developer. Work included creating an OS/2 EE/ES DM-SQL-based object store, and object management of LAN and host-based connectivities. Beta tested VPM 2.0. Attendee: Digitalk Development Conference 97.

Bit Stream Technology, Scottsdale, Arizona
Principal/System Developer, 05/02–10/03
Formed company to utilize object-oriented technology in building model-based software application systems. The focus was on both consulting and application delivery, with the language vehicles being Smalltalk/VPM/VW and C++. Development included an object description and management class system that facilitated rapid application development, especially with graphically based simulations. Specific application development was engineering related.

CH2M Hill, Denver, Colorado
Systems Analyst/Micro Software Development,
Corporate Information Systems, 01/98–04/02
Lead corporate developer for microcomputer software system and application design and programming with the emphasis on creating an application development platform of re-usable high-level DBMS and interface components. The systems architecture was object oriented in construction with event-driven processing. It included a spreadsheet user interface and data-serving communications, both asynch and Ethernet.

References on Request

Carver J. Wood, P.C.E.

225 W. Vine Lane • Atwood, Tennessee 38220 • (615) 555-2294
carverwood@xxx.com

Professional Experience—Computer Systems Engineering

Vashon-Wells, Westport, Connecticut
Systems and Application Programmer
Graphics Products Center
07/02 to 1/05
Worked on a program for a systems-level architecture for graphics products. The first four months of employment involved planning the data structures and user interface for a redesign of one of the graphics products—the map-making software MAP-MASTER.

VRAM Systems Inc., Cambridge, Massachusetts
Systems Analyst/Software Engineer
10/00 to 04/02
Lead designer of DBM in CAD/DBM system. An integrated CAD/database system was created with the DBM residing in a custom windowing system. The primary market for the system is architectural design and drafting. Languages: C++ and COBOL.

07/00 to 09/00
Assisted in planning a new architectural CAD system. Participated in creating system definition/design requirements. Evaluated HP-UX 3.xx on Series 200 hardware as well as Sun Microsystem hardware/Berkeley Unix. Tested the IBM PC AT and various C compilers.

01/00 to 06/00
Ported relational DBM/application development system. I licensed to SKOK a DBMS I developed. The system was ported from an IBM PC to Hewlett-Packard Series 200 equipment (68000 based) using the Pascal Operating System. The system was marketed for $8,000 per user license as ARBASE. Languages: BP-Pascal and 68000 assembler.

Zen Tech Microsystems, Acton, Massachusetts
Principal/Developer
07/98 to 11/99
Formed company to design, implement, and distribute a state-of-the-art DBM/application development system for 16-bit microcomputers. The principal market for the system was the small business user. As of 1999 the system was being marketed by four companies in Massachusetts. A source license was sold to SKOK for use in conjunction with their architectural CAD system.

Page 1 of 2

Professional Experience *(continued)*
Edge Data Corporation, Cambridge, Massachusetts
Microsystems Department Manager
10/97 to 06/98
Worked as a consultant in the design of software and the designation of hardware requirements for high-end microcomputer systems. Programming was done in Pascal and 8086 assembler.

HH Aerospace Design Co. Inc., Bedford/Cambridge, Massachusetts
Consulting Programmer
02/97 to 09/97
Worked on a team modifying the ARTS IIIA air traffic control system to include a conflict alert capability as specified by FAA contract. The program was done in UNIVAC ULTRA assembly language on a real-time, multi-processing system of seven IOP processors.

Professional Experience—Other Fields
Center High School, Hadley, Missouri
Teacher
08/93 to 08/94
Instructed all high school mathematics classes.

Adult Education Center, East St. Louis, Illinois
Instructor
01/87 to 08/89
Developed a curriculum in mathematics for a complete, intensive high school–level course, which was later adopted by a local junior college.

Education
B.S., Computer Engineering, Wentworth Institute, Boston, Massachusetts
• Graduated first in a class of 180 in college; captain of the tennis team.

Additional Information
• Maintain a strong interest in the uses of microcomputer technology.
• Active in developing investment software applications for personal use.
• Prior member of the Boston Computer Society.
• Travel—Australia, New Zealand, Cook Islands, Tahiti.

References provided on request.

THOMAS K. LEWIS

Route 3, Box 112-5 • Big Timber, MT 59011
(406) 555-4730 • thomaslewis@xxx.com

EDUCATION

Bachelor of Science, Computer Integrated Manufacturing Technology, Purdue
University, West Lafayette, IN
May 2000, GPA: 3.2/4.0.

New Castle Area Vocational School, New Castle, IN
1993 - 1994, 1994 - 1995; Vocational Welding
Honors: Outstanding Welder of the Year (both years), president of local
V.I.C.A. chapter (both years).
1995 - 1996; Industrial Cooperative Training (I.C.T.)
Honors: Outstanding Employee of the Year.

EXPERIENCE

Aisin U.S.A. Mfg., Inc. 3/03 - Present
Quality Assurance Engineer
• Automotive Customers Quality Representative.
• Manufacturing/quality planning functions.
• Manage multiple projects for new and existing products.
• Gauge and fixturing design/procurement.
• Attended training sessions for QS 9000.

Major Tool and Machine, Inc.   6/98 - 3/03
Quality Assurance Engineer (5/01 - 3/03)
• Managed quality operations for branch office.
• Manufacturing/quality planning functions.
• Coordinated measuring machine operation/inspection.
• Facilitator for ISO 9000 certification.

Manufacturing Engineer (5/00 - 5/01)
• Process Engineer.
• CAD design of welding and machining fixturing.
• Coordinated the Suggestion Program.

Quality Assurance Inspector (6/98 - 5/00)
• Interpreted customer purchase orders and blueprint requirements.
• Inspected and evaluated part characteristics.
• Organized quality packets and ensured accuracy/completeness.

MILITARY

Cavalry Scout/Unit Armorer, United States Army, August 1996 - June 1998

References on request.

Amelia Gomez-Nacio

227 N.W. 15th Street • Phoenix, Arizona 85021
602-555-9930 • Ameliagomez-nacio@xxx.com

Position Objective

Aeronautical engineering position with major aeronautics laboratory.

Previous Employment

Aerodynamics Engineering Technician
Satellite Operations Center, Scottsdale, Arizona
June 2002 to August 2004
Responsibilities Included:

• Involvement in aero/thermal engineering, aerodynamics, thermodynamics, and fluid mechanics programs. Testing low-speed incompressible to hypersonic flows in both analytical and experimental developments. Prepared system concept studies, detailed analyses. Monitored laboratory and wind tunnel testing and flight testing. Specific projects included the development and testing of hypersonic reentry configurations, gas-dynamic laser flow facilities, aerodynamic control of high-power laser propagation, and the analysis and measurement of aerodynamic phenomena affecting the performance of ground-based and airborne sensors.

Engineering Intern

Los Alamos Laboratory and Testing Center, Los Alamos, New Mexico
June to September 2001
Responsibilities Included:

• Assisting aerodynamics, electronics, mechanical, and astronautical engineers in varying aspects of testing assessment and analysis. Role on team was primarily as observer. Participated in planning and design meetings. Maintained record-keeping files for three departmental engineers.

Education

2004: Master of Science, Aeronautics Engineering, University of Nevada, Las Vegas
2002: Bachelor of Science, Aeronautics Engineering, Embry-Riddle Aeronautical University, Daytona Beach, Florida

References

Available on request.

))) Stuart G. Davies

22785 S.E. Bascomb Road
Rogue River, Oregon 97502
(503) 555-9112
stuartdavies@xxx.com

))) Professional Objective

Forest Engineering position with major timber corporation.

))) Educational Background

Bachelor of Science Degree, Forest Engineering/Civil Engineering, University of the Southwest, Phoenix, Arizona.
Degree awarded December 2003; graduated 6th in class of 120.

))) Areas of Academic Training

) **Forest Transportation Systems:** Analysis of interactions between harvesting and road systems. Road and landing spacing, determination of road standards, analysis of logging road networks, transfer and sort yard facility location. Simultaneous resource scheduling and transportation planning. Fixed and variable transportation cost economics as applied to transportation issues.

) **Logging Mechanics:** Relationship of torque, power, and thrust to the operation of cable and ground harvesting systems. Fundamentals of cable logging system performance, properties of wire rope, load-tension relationships, payload calculation, and carriage design. Analysis of lateral yarding and slack-pulling forces, guyline production and spar tree analysis, interlock design, estimating, production using physical models.

) **Forest Engineering Operations Management:** Harvest unit optimization; optimization of equipment replacement, scheduling, and selection. Applied analysis using linear programming, integer programming, dynamic programming, network techniques, non-linear programming, iterative techniques, and simulation. Identification and measurement of production components in harvesting systems, heavy equipment operations, and crew-type activities. Methods analysis, productivity improvement, and engineering economics. Strategic planning of transportation systems using network theory. Writing reports and oral presentation.

) **Production Planning:** Resource planning using critical path analysis, linear programming, and tactical approaches. Analysis of alternatives using benefit foregone, intangibles, and regulations. Business planning, including bidding, budgeting, scheduling, inventory control, equipment replacement analysis, and fleet maintenance.

❱❱❱ Areas of Academic Training *(continued)*

❱ **Forest Surveying:** Plane surveying using forestry problems. Low-order surveying with compass, abney, clinometer, and hand level. U.S. Public Land Survey System, topography, and mapping. Directional instruments, electronic distance measurements, field astronomy, State Plane Coordinate Systems, horizontal control, specifications, triangulation, and trilateration. Survey law.

❱❱❱ Previous Work Experience

Timber worker, Johnson Brothers Logging Co., Rogue River, Oregon, 1997 to 2001. Experienced with all areas of logging operation, including felling, yarding, slack pulling, guyline, spar setting, and loading.

❱ References provided upon request.
❱ Course transcripts also available.

PAT WAHANA 445 W. Fifth Street
Raleigh, North Carolina 27612
(919) 555-4820
patwahana@xxx.com

OBJECTIVE: Industrial Engineering Management

EXPERIENCE: Industrial Engineer
E-Systems, Inc., ECI Division, Raleigh, North Carolina
2002 to present
Responsibilities include:
• Design and initiate all stages of production process.
• Design and installation of assembly lines and procedures.
• Automated production and testing.
• Experienced with most advanced testing equipment
  currently available.
• Quality control operations; ensure products and systems
  meet required specifications.
• Analyze failures or defects to determine necessary
  corrective measures.
• Installation, maintenance, and modernization of plant
  facilities.

Industrial Engineer
Emerson Electric Co., St. Louis, Missouri
2000 to 2002
Responsibilities included:
• All phases of production, budgeting, and scheduling.
• All aspects of procurement and planning for manufactur-
  ing areas.
• Testing and troubleshooting of manufacturing processes.
• Training of new engineering hires.

EDUCATION: B.S., Industrial Engineering
Wake Technical Institute, Raleigh, North Carolina
Degree awarded June 2000

MEMBERSHIPS: Society of Women Engineers, North Carolina Chapter
American Institute of Plant Engineers
American Institute of Industrial Engineers
North Carolina Association of Industrial Engineers

REFERENCES: Provided upon request

Miguel Sifuentes

3290 S.W. Arches Street • Pueblo, CO 81030 • (303) 555-2286
miguelsifuentes@xxx.com

Job Objective
Mechanical Engineering position with major manufacturing corporation.

Related Work Experience
Mechanical Engineer
Allied Industrial Systems
Pueblo, CO
January 1994 to November 2004

> Responsible for all phases of mechanical design and development of sophisticated equipment used in transportation--from ships to space shuttles. High level of accuracy essential. Oversaw production design with industrial engineers. Worked with production chief to determine optimal methods for production. Assisted with departmental budget preparation and implementation.
> • Plant closed November 2004.

Mechanical Engineer
AN/APO, Inc., Government and Defense Group
Denver, CO
June 1993 to January 1994

> Responsible for variety of duties on physical design projects, including airborne, shipborne, or land. Handled stress analysis, fracture analysis, and product improvement design of all the electromechanical servomechanisms. Designed hydraulic systems, performed testing, and prepared specifications and proposals. Worked closely with electrical and manufacturing engineers and technicians.

Technician
Mechanical Engineering Division AN/APO, Inc., Industrial Group
Denver, CO
June 1990 to June 1993

> Worked half-time while completing training for Professional Mechanical Engineer Certificate. Assisted mechanical and manufacturing engineers with analyses, testing, and mechanical drafting.

Education
B.S., Mechanical Engineering, June 1990
Pueblo University, Pueblo, CO

Professional Mechanical Engineer Certificate, June 1993
American Society of Mechanical Engineers, State of Colorado, Denver, CO

References available on request.

Jake Markham

443 W. Emerson Drive • Concord, New Hampshire 03301

(603) 555-8991 • jakemarkham@xxx.com

Employment Objective

Seeking a position as a senior electronics engineer with a company involved with the design of electronic systems.

Work Experience

Electronics Engineer, J&G Industrial Electronics, Inc.
Concord, New Hampshire
June 2001 to present
Responsibilities include: Design hardware; interface, test, analyze, and evaluate microprocessors. Operate, design, and test microcomputer-based instrumentation systems. Research automatic test systems, radar systems, and guidance systems. Research performance statistics on complete systems. Work with both analog and digital systems.

Digital Electronics Engineer, Digital Enterprises of New Hampshire
Manchester, New Hampshire
June 1999 to June 2001
Responsibilities included: Design digital circuitry on microprocessor applications, high-speed multiprocessor computer architecture, digital signal processors, and bit-mapped graphics. Concerned with real-time applications, micro-programming, assembly language, and high-level language. Special projects involved image processing, signal/data processing, control/servo systems, test systems, and artificial intelligence. Contributed to projects on fire control systems and electronic intelligence devices.

Education

Bachelor of Science Degree, Electronics Engineering
University of Manchester, New Hampshire
Degree awarded June 1999
Served as president of student chapter of Institute of Electrical and Electronics Engineers for two years. Actively involved in Engineering Honor Society, organizing speakers and presentations by faculty on special topics. Coordinated placement assistance program for electrical and electronics engineering students in cooperation with career counseling department on the campus.

References provided on request.

DANIEL EVANS CREIGHTON

1442 S. Jefferson Street
Brattleboro, Vermont 05351
(802) 555-6648
danielevanscreighton@xxx.com

OBJECTIVE

Position as ceramic engineer with manufacturing corporation

PREVIOUS EMPLOYMENT

Ceramic Engineer, Champion Spark Plug Company, Toledo, Ohio
Employment Dates: August 2000 to January 2004
Involved in the development of new ceramic bodies, materials processing, and quality controls for the development and production of spark plug insulators. Conducted studies on glass, semiconductors, glazes, high-temperature sealants, and cements. Developed strategy for testing procedures that saved 15 percent in costs annually and increased testing accuracy and efficiency by 45 percent.

Materials Engineer, Avco Systems, Textron, Wilmington, Massachusetts
Employment Dates: September 1996 to July 2000
Developed advanced materials for heat protection systems applications. Synthesized plastic, ceramic, and graphite composite constructions, including high-temperature processing procedures. Responsible for analysis, reliability, maintainability, safety, planning, and conducting all formal system-level testing.

EDUCATIONAL BACKGROUND

Bachelor of Science, Materials Engineering, University of Massachusetts, Amherst
Degree Date: August 1996

Graduate course work completed in Ceramics Engineering, University of Toledo
Enrollment Dates: September 2000 to June 2002
Completed 65 percent of work required for Master of Science degree

MEMBERSHIPS

- American Ceramic Society
- American Society for Testing and Materials
- Ohio Council for Industrial Engineers (former)
- Engineering Society of Massachusetts (former)

References on Request

Jane Bessington

18 West Court Street • Shreveport, Louisiana 71102 • (318) 555-6510
janebessington@xxx.com

Objective
Electronics Engineering position with innovative communications corporation.

Education
Bachelor's Degree in Electronics Engineering
University of Louisiana, Baton Rouge
Degree Awarded 2002

Engineer-In-Training
ACI and Associates, New Orleans, Louisiana
Certification/License Pending

Occupational Experience
Electronics Engineer Technician (Engineer-In-Training)
ACI and Associates, New Orleans, Louisiana
June 2002 to June 2003
Responsibilities included:
• Testing of electro-optical analog and digital processors.
• Review of design and technology for microprocessors.
• Analysis of signal processing identification and warning systems.
• Digital analysis study preparation.
• Assisting with testing and predictions of mean-time-between-failure rates (MTBF).
• Assisting electronics engineers in preparation of components.
• Attending training sessions in electronics engineering for the professional.

Memberships
• Institute for Electrical and Electronics Engineers, Student Chapter, ULBR
• ULBR Engineering Honor Society
• Student Coalition for Responsible Science and Engineering

References
Available upon request.
Official university transcripts also provided on request.

Abdul Gassazi Murza

224 West Fourth Street
Albany, New York 12211
(518) 555-6428
abdulgassazimurza@xxx.com

Position Desired

Aeromechanics engineering position with manufacturer of commercial or military aircraft. Willing to relocate anywhere in the United States.

Education

M.S., Aerodynamics and Engineering Design, 2004
Wentworth Institute, Boston, Massachusetts

B.S., Aeromechanics Engineering, 2001
Kansas Technical Institute, Salina, Kansas

Areas Studied
- Dynamics: Aeroelastic loads and stability. Dynamic test and evaluation.
- Aerodynamics: Aerodynamic and performance analysis. Preliminary design analysis. Wind tunnel test program design. Development of aerodynamics analysis tools.
- Stability and Control: Qualities analysis and design. Flight simulation testing design and analysis. Development of real-time simulation models. Integration of feedback for advanced flight control laws.
- Structural Dynamics: Test vibrations, dynamics loads. Aeroelastic stability of materials. Layout and design of mechanical structure materials, parts, and components.

Experience

Research Associate: Under Dr. Malcolm Fisher, Research & Development Department, Wentworth Institute, Boston, Massachusetts, 2001–2004
- Conducted research and experimentation on aeroelastic properties of various materials. Prepared detailed reports on test results. Analyzed data sets with linear and non-linear methodology. Assisted with writing of final report for publication.

References

References, publications, and transcripts will be provided upon request.

K. J. BUTTERS • 2276 La Center Boulevard • Gainesville, FL 32601
(352) 555-7765 • kjbutters@xxx.com

OBJECTIVE   Quality control management position in the energy industry, prefer-
ably hydroelectric power or solar power development.

EXPERIENCE   **Quality Control Supervisor**
Florida Power & Electric, Nuclear Division
Gainesville, FL, June 2002 to present
- Program planning and data evaluation; quality control supervision
  in all areas of operation, design, and production in compliance with
  the requirements of the Nuclear Regulatory Commission and other
  regulatory agencies.
- Assist in licensing review activities and coordinate all licensing
  aspects of projects.
- Thermal analysis, thermal/fluid dynamics analysis of water, gas,
  and liquid-cooled reactor cores.
- Random testing and evaluation of instrumentation control.
- Evaluation and testing of operations procedures and safety
  procedures.
- Supervise staff of seven engineers and five engineering technicians.
- Cooperate with nuclear engineers in testing and maintenance
  programs.
- Provide quality assurance training to all new operators.
- Coordinate safety and quality control communications for seven
  reactor facilities.

Nuclear Engineer
Florida Power & Electric, Nuclear Division
Orlando, FL, June 1998 to June 2002
- Thermal analysis and thermal/fluid dynamics design and testing.
- Design and testing of reactor core components.
- Systems design and analysis.
- Manage activities of the maintenance department and provide
  technical supervision to ensure the safe, reliable, and efficient
  operation of the nuclear plant.
- Review, investigate, analyze, and interpret data on costs, man-
  power, materials, and schedules in support of project management.

EDUCATION   B.S., Nuclear Engineering, 1998
Pennsylvania State University, Altoona

References provided on request.

JAMES P. ARCHER

12267 W. STARKER DRIVE • LACENTER, WASHINGTON 98629
(206) 555-0029 • JAMESARCHER@XXX.COM

POSITION OBJECTIVE
Mechanical engineering position in construction or manufacturing.

PROFESSIONAL EXPERIENCE
Mechanical Engineer
Washington Pacific Power Supply Corporation
Seattle, Washington
1999 to present

Coordinate additions to and alterations and retirements of corporate facilities. Serve as consultant on design, construction, and operating problems. Make engineering studies and assist with research and development plans to achieve the most economical expansion of the corporation's physical plant operations in the mechanical engineering fields. Inspect and conduct tests on mechanical equipment to determine if it meets the required specifications. Responsible for quality control of construction operation at two new plant sites.

Mechanical Engineering Specialist
Bonneville Power Station
Bonneville, Oregon
1996 to 1999

Coordinated power plant loading. Analyzed plant efficiency and cost data to effect optimum use of facilities in power production. Operated, maintained, and measured performance of on-line power stations along Columbia River. Worked as instrumentation and control engineer as needed for relief.

EDUCATION
B.S., Mechanical Engineering
University of Washington, Seattle
Awarded June 1996

Special Training in Energy Engineering, Safety Control, Quality Assurance, and Engineering Economics through American Institute of Mechanical Engineers.

MEMBERSHIPS
• American Institute of Mechanical Engineers
• Association of Energy Engineers
• Northwest Energy Engineers Coalition

References on request.

Gerald McCraig, P.E.

2259 Queen Street SE
Allentown, PA 18101
(814) 555-2293
geraldmccraig@xxx.com

Career Goal
Senior Electrical Engineering position within the energy production industry.

Employment Experience
2001–present
Electrical Engineer
Pennsylvania Power & Light Company, Allentown, PA
Assist in preparation of plans for development and expansion of company facilities operations. Development, design, and implementation of computer procedures that apply engineering and mathematical techniques to solving complex technical problems. Planning, design, and construction supervision of three new electrical facilities. Reviewing plants for potential improvements. Preparing plans, designs, and maintenance schedules to implement improvements. Experienced with instrumentation control engineering for operation of boilers, turbines, and other power plant (non-nuclear) equipment. Perform and direct electrical tests required to place and maintain in service the automatic and manual control distribution systems in the eastern Pennsylvania territory. Plan, schedule, and conduct voltage surveys. Operate, maintain, and measure the performance of on-line power stations.

1998–2001
Engineer-In-Training
Pennsylvania Power & Light Company, Allentown, PA
Worked as special assistant to senior electrical engineer during work in training program toward licensing and certification. Assisted with all aspects of electrical engineering work in power generation and relay stations.

Education
1997
B.S. in Electrical Engineering
University of Pennsylvania, Allentown

Memberships
Institute of Electrical and Electronics Engineers
Society of Pennsylvania Electrical Engineers

References on request.

Patrick J. Allen

17 East Moreland Drive
Chicago, Illinois 60611
patrickallen@xxx.com

Tel: (312) 555-2298
Fax: (312) 555-2192

Registration:

- Licensed Professional Engineer, State of Illinois
- Certified Environmental Professional, National

Recent Accomplishments:

- Served as project manager for the successful completion of a comprehensive integrated solid waste management project for Will County, south of Chicago.
- Assisted in the preparation and implementation of a land use development plan for the State of Illinois, in cooperation with the Land Development Commission, the Environmental Protection League, and the Federal Bureau of Land Management.
- Prepared and directed engineering feasibility study, including environmental impact statement, for sifting of water treatment facility.

Employment History:

1999 - 2004   Templeton Engineering Consultants, Inc.
452 East Stewart Avenue, Suite 112
Chicago, Illinois 60612
Senior Engineering Consultant

1997 - 1999   M.W.N. Engineering Associates, Ltd.
Parker Building, Suite 2600
24th and Madison
Chicago, Illinois 60602
Engineer-Hydrologist

1993 - 1997   Tensor Industries, Inc.
144 West Marquam
Chicago, Illinois 60626
Engineering Technician

Education:

1993   L.P.E. Course, Illinois Institute of Technology, Chicago
1992   B.S., Geological Engineering, Wheaton College, Wheaton, Illinois

References: Upon request

JARRED W. CONLIFF

4644 Southwest Marine Drive   (810) 555-3488
Stoneybrook, California 94311   FAX (810) 555-3498
jarredconliff@xxx.com

OBJECTIVE

Seeking a position in waste control engineering with responsibility for facilities management.

QUALIFICATIONS SUMMARY

Petrophysical engineer with strengths in treatment and disposal of hazardous and toxic waste, analyzing natural and occupational environments for pollution, managing waste remediation, planning disposal and treatment of hazardous waste, designing and operating air and water pollution control equipment, and administering waste management systems.

PROFESSIONAL EXPERIENCE

California-Pacific Power Company   1997 to present
La Jolla, California
General Field Engineer

- Managed hazardous waste remediation program for nuclear waste water from four facilities.
- Designed water pollution control units for relay stations.
- Earned three promotions in four years through corporate training and development programs.
- Established computerized tracking system for waste removal program.
- Monitored air and water pollution levels for three-county territory.
- Developed and implemented plans for corrective measures on air and water emissions.
- Voluntarily instituted tougher standards for emissions.
- Trained field engineers in pollution evaluation and control.

PROFESSIONAL EXPERIENCE (continued)

American Marine Drilling Corporation   1995 to 1997
San Diego, California
Engineering Technician
- Responsible for designing and directing drilling operations from start-up to dismantling.
- Trained in hazardous waste shipping and chemical containment.
- Monitored marine geophysical research reports and incorporated relevant information into design and operations plans.

EDUCATION

B.S., Petrophysical Engineering   1995
Colorado Institute of Mineral Science and Technology
Mountain Park, Colorado

REFERENCES ON REQUEST

Hunter Bottjer

2254 W. Brick Street, Apt. B4

Anchorage, Alaska 99510

(907) 555-2247 • hunterbottjer@xxx.com

Professional Objective

To achieve an associate-level management position in the drafting department of a major mechanical engineering firm.

Experience

Assistant Manager, Product Engineering, Drafting Division
Aleutian-Pacific Engineering, Inc.
Anchorage, Alaska • June 2001 to present
Supervise production drafting of engine parts for large-engine manufacturing company. Responsible for assessing and approving the quality of drafting by 14 full-time drafters. Saved the company $1.2 million in projected revenue loss by detecting design flaw in a major engine component.

Senior Drafter, Product Engineering, Drafting Division
Aleutian-Pacific Engineering, Inc.
Anchorage, Alaska • April 2000 to June 2001
Drafting high-voltage power switching equipment to customer specifications and structures. Responsible for drafting component of major engine redesign in team-managed project.

Drafter I & Drafter II, Product Engineering, Drafting Division
Aleutian-Pacific Engineering, Inc.
Anchorage, Alaska • June 1997 to April 2000

Assistant Manager, Winter Creek Building Supply
Galena, Alaska • February 1993 to September 1995
Assisted in start-up of building supply firm in retail and wholesale sales, government sales, purchasing, and inventory control.

Education

Associate's Degree, Mechanical Engineering
Kitsap Community College
Kitsap, Washington • June 1997

References Available

JONATHAN HOOPER

7728 S. Coruna Street • Santa Fe, NM 87502
(505) 555-2497 • jonathanhooper@xxx.com

OBJECTIVE

Project management position with an engineering technologies consulting firm.

SUMMARY OF QUALIFICATIONS

Expertise in the areas of waste-to-energy and waste recovery technology solutions, recycling technology, testing and analysis of groundwater levels and flow, and electric power generation technologies. Excellent written and oral communications skills and thorough knowledge of current environmental regulations for federal and state policy makers.

RECENT PROJECT EXPERIENCE

- Project Manager, Santa Fe Environmental Systems Waste-to-Energy Feasibility Study-- Preparation of an analysis of the solid waste management practices of the Santa Fe regional facility, coupled with an environmental assessment of a potential site to determine the feasibility of developing a waste-to-energy facility in Lamy, NM. Developed engineering design for facility currently under construction.
- Consultant/Project Manager, Department of Sanitation, Santa Fe--Preparation of a feasibility study (environmental fatal flaws, geotechnical analysis, engineering constraints, hydrogeologic analysis) for the proposed redevelopment of the closed San Felipe Landfill for use as an ash residue disposal site for the city's solid waste incinerators and proposed waste-to-energy facilities.
- Project Engineer, Southeast Project, Santa Fe--Development of engineering design and permit information for development of a major fossil-fuel–fired electric generating facility.
- Lead Environmental Analyst, County Energy Management Committee, Santa Fe--Designed study to perform environmental impact comparative analysis of current coal generators versus waste-to-energy incinerator-generators. Study published in national professional journal.

WORK HISTORY

2002–present:	Consultant, Enso Engineering Associates, Santa Fe, NM
1998–2002:	Hydrologist, New Mexico Department of Energy, Albuquerque, NM
1995–1998:	Research Associate, University of New Mexico, Albuquerque, NM

EDUCATION

1995:	Bachelor's Degree in Hydrology Engineering, University of New Mexico, Albuquerque
1990:	Professional Engineer License Examination Completed

References Available on Request

TRENT HOWARD
149 N.E. Goshen Drive
Fredericksburg, VA 22405
(703) 555-6265
trenthoward@xxx.com

EMPLOYMENT OBJECTIVE
Engineering consultant for water resources management organization.

EDUCATION
M.S., Water Resources Engineering
Virginia Technical Institute, 2003

B.S., Civil Engineering (Minor in Water Resource Engineering)
Purdue University, 2000

WORK HISTORY AND EXPERIENCE
Research Associate, Virginia Technical Institute, 2000 to present
Hired as associate to Research and Consulting Division of VTI, working on a variety of special projects, including:
• Georgia Rivers Study: Navigability investigation of the streams and rivers within the civil works area; under contract to the U.S. Army Corps of Engineers, Savannah, Georgia.
• Alaska Rivers Study: Navigability investigation of the streams and rivers crossed by the Trans-Alaska Oil Pipeline; under contract to the U.S. Army Corps of Engineers, Alaska District.
• Wetlands Study: A comparative analysis of methods of identifying freshwater wetlands; under contract to the U.S. Army Corps of Engineers, Adirondack District.
• Upper Roanoke River Basin Study: Navigability, water flow, and water quality investigation of waters of the Upper Roanoke River Basin; under contract to the State of Virginia, Department of Water Resources.
• Headwater Pilot Program: Hydrologic analysis of small headwater streams to determine selection of location along the Upper James River, Virginia; under contract to the State of Virginia, Department of Water Resources.

MEMBERSHIPS
Water Resources Institute of Virginia
American Water Resources Association

Complete references will be provided on request.

◗◗◗ Wallace D. Mamaka

334 Terra Lane • Denver, Colorado 80212 • (303) 555-6675
wallacemamaka@xxx.com

◗ Employment Objective

Engineering specialist position with responsibility for permitting procedures for mining corporation.

◗ Relevant Experience

- ◗ Developed a program for the reclamation of boreholes and excavations for feasibility of developing a coal mine.
- ◗ Conducted site analysis and prepared list of permit requirements for development of major oil shale project.
- ◗ Prepared a historical summary of heavy oil mining efforts and comparison of present-day methods.
- ◗ Coordinated environmental-impact analysis and drafted statement for development of a 25-acre sand and gravel mining operation.
- ◗ Prepared a hard-rock mining reclamation plan with applicable permit documents and supplemented with traffic and noise studies.
- ◗ Instituted permit procedures for the relocation (excavation and filling) of soil within a 100-year flood plain for designated recreational river corridor.

◗ Employment History

Mining Engineer, Sandview Mining Corporation
Denver, Colorado, 1999 to present

Engineering Technician, Mobil Oil
Denver, Colorado, 1996 to 1999
Los Angeles, California, 1994 to 1996

◗ Education

Colorado State University, Fort Collins
M.S., Mining and Metallurgy Technology, 1994
B.S., Geology, 1992

◗ References

Provided on request.

Regina B. Hernandez

19087 Shadowcrest Ave.
Louisville, CO 80027
(303) 555-9876
reginahernandez@xxx.com

Degrees Conferred:

Ph.D. in Material Science and Engineering, University of Colorado, 2005
M.S. in Material Science and Engineering, University of Colorado, 2003
B.A. in Chemistry, University of Colorado, 2000

Experience:

Summer 2003
Assistant Physicist
General Aircraft Corporation, Boulder, CO

Summer 2000
Graduate Research Assistant
Department of Materials Science and Engineering
University of Colorado
Research Topic:
Stress Corrosion Cracking in Aircalory Nuclear Fuel Cladding—
Accelerated SCC Testing of Cladding, Chemical Compatibility

Summer 1999
Undergraduate Research Project
Department of Chemical Engineering
University of Colorado
Research Topic:
Design of Equipment to Be Used to Study the
Coating of a Rotating Surface with a Viscous Fluid

REFERENCES AVAILABLE

Donald E. Henry
3125 Cool Creek Drive
Carmel, IN 46032
(317) 555-9406

Objective   To obtain a position as an engineer with the opportunity to apply my knowledge of digital circuit design, programmable controllers, and microprocessors.

Employment   July 2003 to Present
Allied Wholesale Electrical Supply Inc.
Indianapolis, IN
Systems Engineer
Responsibilities Include:
• Resolving computer problems
• Keeping inventory
• Working with programmable controllers
• Working with CAD
• Analyzing change requests
• Writing troubleshooting documentation

August 2000 to June 2003
Webber Engineering
Carmel, IN
Die Detailer
Responsibilities Included:
• Drawing and dimensioning die details
• Making engineering changes to die drawings
• Running blueprints

Education   Lawrence Institute of Technology, Southfield, MI
B.S., Electrical Engineering, 2000
Passed Professional Engineering Exam, June 2000

References will be provided upon request.

MARTHA K. BYE

22 Verra Drive • Iowa City, Iowa 52242 • (319) 555-3546 • marthabye@xxx.com

OBJECTIVE

An entry-level position in construction management that will allow me to utilize my technical, organizational, and interpersonal skills to assist with project control tasks.

EDUCATION

Buena Vista College, Storm Lake, Iowa
Department of Civil Engineering
Master of Science Degree, May 2004
Construction Engineering and Management

University of Iowa, Iowa City, Iowa
School of Civil and Environmental Engineering
Bachelor of Science Degree, May 2002
Civil Engineering

Coursework
- Construction Project Organization and Control
- Construction Management
- Legal Aspects of the Construction Process
- Decision Analysis in Construction
- Risk Analysis and Management
- Engineering Economics and Management
- Building Construction and Engineering
- Heavy Construction and Earthwork
- Concrete Materials and Construction
- Civil Engineering Materials
- Structural Engineering
- Geotechnical Engineering
- Transportation Engineering
- Highway Engineering

EXPERIENCE

Research Assistant
January 2002–Present
Buena Vista College
Storm Lake, Iowa

Researched several design- and construction-related areas of bituminous materials as part of the Strategic Highway Research Program sponsored by the Federal Highway Administration. Published an industry-wide report covering the entire scope of this research.

Staff Engineer
May 2000–August 2001
Schnabel Engineering Associates
Denver, Colorado

Assisted in the preparation of a complete operation and maintenance manual for a leachate treatment plant and provided support in the compilation and review of all operation- and maintenance-related submittals from the general contractor and all subcontractors.

ACHIEVEMENTS

- Engineer-in-Training (EIT) Certification
- Dean's List, College of Engineering, Buena Vista College
- Dean's List, College of Engineering, University of Iowa

SKILLS

- Computer Languages: FORTRAN, Pascal, BASIC, C++
- Software: Lotus, SuperCalc, Excel, SAS, AutoCAD, MS Word, MacWrite/WriteNow, Harvard Graphics
- Fluency in German

MEMBERSHIPS

- Student Member, American Society of Civil Engineers
- Student Member, American Concrete Institute

REFERENCES

Available upon request

JUDITH W. SWENSEN

4422 Kennet Avenue • Jubal, Tennessee 37232 • (615) 555-4876
judithswensen@xxx.com

SUMMARY OF QUALIFICATIONS

Experience in providing comprehensive environmental assistance to mining operations and exploration projects. Maintain an awareness of all federal environmental regulations to assess compliance of subsidiary companies. Conduct detailed environmental audits at mining and terminal locations.

ACCOMPLISHMENTS

SOLID WASTE DISPOSAL

As disposal methods analyst, charged with determining best disposal method at each subsidiary mine. Methods chosen are site-specific and depend on depth to groundwater, percentage and types of heavy metals present in the coal ash, and column leachate test results.

Investigated and designed economical solid and hazardous waste disposal options for subsidiary companies.

MINE DRAINAGE TREATMENT

Assisted subsidiaries with effective economical methods of controlling acid mine drainage from coal refuse piles and ensuring reclamation success.

Conducted research with Tennessee State University to determine methods of refuse pretreatment to eliminate future AMD and have successfully installed two systems.

EMPLOYMENT HISTORY

Senior Development Specialist, 2002 to present
Smoky Mountain Mining Company, Memphis, Tennessee

Graduate Assistant/Lab Technician, 1999 to 2002
University of Tennessee, Chemical Engineering Department

EDUCATION

University of Tennessee
Ph.D. in Chemical Engineering, 2002
B.S. in Chemistry and Physics, 1999

References provided on request.

Chapter 6

Sample Cover Letters

This chapter contains sample cover letters for people pursuing a wide variety of jobs and careers in engineering, or who already have experience in this field.

There are many different styles of cover letters in terms of layout, level of formality, and presentation of information. These samples also represent people with varying amounts of education and work experience. Choose one cover letter or borrow elements from several different cover letters to help you construct your own.

17 West Barley Mow
Boston, Massachusetts 02129
tamanaclarendon@xxx.com

February 8, 20__

Mr. John Patterson
Director of Personnel
Hall, Winston & Merck, Architects
2251 W. Pyncheon
Boston, Massachusetts 02113

Dear Mr. Patterson:

In the January 30 edition of the *Globe*, your firm ran an ad for a Construction Inspector Trainee. I submit the enclosed resume and letters of reference in application for this position.

I hold a Bachelor of Science degree in Civil Engineering Technology from the Massachusetts Institute of Technology. While pursuing my degree, I had the opportunity to study many areas associated with civil engineering, including materials testing (soil, concrete, and asphalt), math (through applied calculus), and construction management.

Along with my education, I have experience working with an architectural/ engineering firm producing site, foundation, and floor plans, as well as roof systems and connection details. Recently, I had the opportunity to assist in the construction of residential and small commercial structures for an independent contractor.

I would like to meet with you to answer any additional questions that you might have regarding my qualifications. I can be reached at the address listed above or at (617) 555-2448 or by email at tamanaclarendon@xxx.com. Thank you, and I look forward to hearing from you soon.

Sincerely,

Tamana Clarendon

Enclosures: Resume
References (3)

ROBERTA LOEB
34 Michigan Drive
Des Moines, IA 50317
robertaloeb@xxx.com
515-555-2624

April 4, 20__

Mr. Joshua Sellwood
Environmental Associates
17 West Hallows Avenue, Suite 334
Des Moines, IA 50309

Dear Mr. Sellwood:

It was very good to talk with you about opportunities with Environmental
Associates. I came away from our discussion feeling as if I'd found an ideal
match for both my interests and qualifications. Enclosed is my resume out-
lining my professional experience, as well as a list of professional references
for your consideration.

As we discussed, I am a registered civil engineer with more than seven years
of civil environmental marketing experience in the environmental construction products industry with Semlar Environmental Systems (Semlar
structural geogrids) and Crown Zellerbach Corporation (nonwoven geotextiles). Prior experience includes nine years as a project/construction
manager for Bechtel Engineering and six years as a project/refinery engineer in the oil industry.

My professional objective now is to gain a regional marketing and/or technical support position within the private sector. I have extensive contacts in
the Midwest with environmental engineering consultants, regulatory agencies, and landfill owners/operators, which will offer the prospect of generating new business for your firm. Thank you kindly for your assistance.
I look forward to talking with you further.

Sincerely,

Roberta Loeb, P.E.

BRANDON NICKERSON, P.E.
667 Hurst Avenue
St. Louis, MO 63121
brandonnickerson@xxx.com
573-555-1156

March 1, 20__

Susan W. Coolidge
Vice President
Simmonds Technology, Inc.
Route 5, Box 1265
St. Louis, MO 63102

Dear Ms. Coolidge:

I am sending you my resume for your consideration for any suitable openings that your firm may have at the present time.

I believe my experience in many facets of the environmental field--including project design, procurement, scheduling, and construction--will allow me to make a significant contribution to your operations. Also, my extensive background in electrical and process control systems has given me a well-rounded understanding of most chemical, thermal, and physical processes.

In addition to my engineering management and technical skills, I have had considerable experience in project development, new business development, and the implementation of new technology. During the past seven years I have also had extensive experience in the solid waste management field with in-depth involvement in medical, industrial, and municipal waste handling, incineration, energy recovery, and pollution control projects.

I am available for immediate employment and can travel extensively or relocate as required. I look forward to hearing from you and learning more about any current openings for which I am qualified. Thank you for your consideration.

Yours sincerely,

Brandon Nickerson

Enclosure: Resume

SHAWN SEELEY

22 W. Davis Street • Saginaw, Michigan 48603
(517) 555-2625 • shawnseeley@xxx.com

February 3, 20__

Abel Maxwell
Senior Engineer
Patterby Industrial, Inc.
345 Frontage Road
Saginaw, Michigan 48602

Dear Mr. Maxwell:

Please accept the enclosed resume as my application for the recently
announced engineering technologist position at Patterby Industrial.

As a recent graduate of the University of Michigan's Engineering
Program in engineering technology, I can assure you that I have been
taught by some of the very best--both among my professors at U of M
and among the professional engineers from major corporations throughout the Midwest who provided on-campus seminars on the latest engineering technology.

As a participant in the annual Engineering Technology Competition,
I won second prize for two consecutive years, and I was part of the team
that won first prize this past year. The competition fosters independence,
innovation, and teamwork. You will find that I am an excellent team
player, but that I have the ability to lead when the situation demands.

I would like to arrange an opportunity to visit Patterby Industrial to see
your operations and learn more about your requirements for this position.
I am eager to match my training and abilities to your needs.

I look forward to hearing from you soon. I can be reached at the number
above most afternoons, and messages can be left at any time. Thank you
for your consideration.

Sincerely,

Shawn Seeley

D A R I U S   G . W .   H A R M S

3485 Plainfield Road
Lincoln, Nebraska 68573
Cell: (402) 555-9287
Email:dariusharms@xxx.com

March 6, 20__

Jonathan Parker
Engineering Division Director
State of Nebraska
P.O. Box 5678
Lincoln, Nebraska 68570

Dear Mr. Parker:

Please accept this letter and the enclosed resume in application for the Engineering Supervisor position announced February 25.

I believe my extensive background in structural and mechanical engineering meets or exceeds the qualifications you are looking for. I have served both as a senior engineer and as an engineering supervisor with responsibility for 120 workers.

I would like to put my expertise and experience to work for the benefit of public works projects, where safety and quality form the guiding values, as stated in your position description. Too often in the corporate world, the demand for higher profit margins takes precedence over innovative developments and worker safety. My experience in this field, however, has given me the ability to achieve desired results in the most efficient manner possible, thus cutting costs *and* increasing productivity, while maintaining worker morale and the highest safety considerations.

Please review the enclosed resume and call me at the number above. I would very much like to talk with you about the position and what my experience can bring to your department.

Yours Truly,

Darius Harms

❖ **Donna Everson** ❖

1233 Mission Street ❖ San Pablo, California 98329
(213) 555-0812 ❖ donnaeverson@xxx.com

May 5, 20__

Personnel Director
Bakersfield & Associates
P.O. Box 123
San Pablo, California 98332

Dear Director:

Please accept the enclosed resume in application for the position of Engineering Sales Specialist, which was advertised in the *San Francisco Chronicle* last week. I've worked as a civil engineer for the past eight years and have gained tremendous insight into the issues involved in marketing engineering services on an international basis.

Earlier in my career, I gained some valuable experience as the Engineering Sales Specialist for Shell Oil Company. In this position, I worked with manufacturers and small-business owners to coordinate efforts for fuel efficiency and cost savings. The marketing and sales program that resulted was the most successful in the company's history.

During my graduate program at MIT, I worked closely with several faculty members in consultation with a major technology manufacturer to recast the company's image and stimulate sales in a slogging economy. The strategic planning sessions with corporate executives provided a tremendous on-the-job training opportunity for me as a graduate student, and the project achieved the desired results.

My inquiries have revealed that your firm has a strong reputation for excellence and innovation that makes me eager to bring my skills in strategic planning and market analysis to work for Bakersfield & Associates.

I would appreciate an opportunity to discuss the position with you further. Please call me at (213) 555-0812, where messages may be left if I am personally unavailable.

Thank you for your consideration.

Sincerely,

Donna Everson

Jane Bessington

18 West Court Street • Shreveport, Louisiana 71102 • (318) 555-6510
janebessington@xxx.com

June 16, 20__

Jane Flanagan
Director of Personnel
AT&T
9595 Mansfield
Shreveport, LA 71130

Dear Ms. Flanagan:

I am writing in response to the advertised electronics engineering position. Please accept the enclosed resume in application.

I was particularly attracted to this position because of my previous experience as an electronics engineering technician with ACI and Associates in New Orleans, where I was officially an Engineer-In-Training while preparing for professional licensing. I have completed all necessary courses and examinations, and will have confirmation of my license by next week.

AT&T's commitment to further educational training is an essential factor in my choosing to apply for this position. The dynamic nature of this field, and the number of individuals working toward new and innovative technology, both within AT&T and in other agencies, means that vast amounts of valuable information need to be reviewed in order to stay on top. I look forward to attending seminars on a regular basis to keep current with this rapidly changing field.

I believe my credentials and commitment to innovation and development make me an excellent candidate for this position. I look forward to talking with you soon.

Sincerely,

Jane Bessington

Abdul Gassazi Murza

224 West Fourth Street
Albany, New York 12211
(518) 555-6428
abdulgassazimurza@xxx.com

February 9, 20__

Dr. Lewis J. Stone, Director
Aeromechanical Engineering Division
McDonnell Douglas Helicopter Company
4645 South Ash Avenue
Tempe, Arizona 85282

Dear Dr. Stone:

After meeting with you at the American Institute of Aeronautics and Astronautics convention last week in Phoenix, I am delighted to write now in application for an entry-level position with your aeromechanics engineering division. Our discussion was most valuable in providing information about McDonnell Douglas's helicopter branch, and I am intrigued to become part of such an exciting operation.

As a graduate student at Boston's Wentworth Institute, my focus was primarily on the design and construction of military jets. I was able to apply the principles of aeronautics and aeromechanics to my work as a research assistant on a project for testing the aeroelasticity of materials for safer, more efficient production of supersonic jets. The project resulted in a patented new technology, which is currently being employed in the construction of several new jets for the U.S. Air Force.

I would like to visit your facilities and talk with you further about what I can bring to this position. If possible, I would appreciate approximately 10 days' notice, so that I can make appropriate travel arrangements.

Thank you for your consideration. I look forward to talking with you again soon.

Best regards,

Abdul Gassazi Murza

2276 La Center Boulevard
Gainesville, FL 32601

June 13, 20__

R. W. Matson
Matson & Carter Enterprises
One Commercial Parkway East
Tampa, FL 32200

Dear Mr. Matson:

In response to your recent advertisement in the *Florida Herald*, I am writing to apply for the position as quality control engineer.

My resume, enclosed, indicates the extensive training and experience I have in the field of quality assurance and quality control. My strengths include an ability to work successfully with people--from top department managers and CEOs to entry-level engineering technicians and production line personnel. I am dependable, dedicated to quality, and have a positive "teamwork" attitude.

My professional experience has primarily been in the nuclear engineering field. The career change from the nuclear industry will enable me to bring a fresh perspective to all of your energy-related clients because of the essential elements of safety and quality control in this exacting field.

I look forward to meeting with you at your earliest convenience. You may reach me at (407) 555-2203, ext. 1945, during working hours, and at (407) 555-3090 evenings and weekends. I can also be reached via email: K.J.Hasson@xxx.com. Thank you for your time and consideration.

Best,

K. J. Hasson

October 8, 20__

Draycott Engineering, Inc.
Center Building Complex
Suite 221
5377 W. Carver
Seattle, WA 98002

To the Director of Personnel:

The enclosed resume and letters of recommendation are being submitted in application for the Assistant Project Manager's position with your company, announced in the September 20 edition of *Seattle Business Week*.

I have recently relocated to the Seattle area and am looking forward to taking on new challenges in my engineering career. Most recently I worked as a public works inspector, primarily involved with inspection of civil engineering projects and assisting with project planning. My previous positions were as an assistant project manager for a major construction corporation and as an engineering technician for a local government agency.

My experience covers all areas of project management, including design, planning, budgeting, scheduling, and personnel management. I am available to travel as required but prefer to keep Seattle as my primary base.

I will call you next week to arrange a time to discuss the position and my credentials with you at greater length. If you have any questions, please call me at the number below. I look forward to hearing from you.

Sincerely,

Susan G. Carter
1983 Madison SE
Bellevue, WA 98008
(206) 555-2283
susancarter@xxx.com